We all agreed that their list was better. That interplay was a spirited moment and influenced the rest of the vacation. However, not all vacations with teens are fun.

Making something out of "dud" vacations

Family vacations can become problematic as kids get older—real duds. Teens are often more reluctant to spend time with family. One way to ease this problem is to join with another family with kids of similar ages or let the kids bring along a friend.

A few years ago our family went to Hawaii for a week. We brought along Matt, a family friend. We called him "the buffer" because he was a friend of both of our boys, and we were hoping that his presence would help reduce the sibling quarreling that was so annoying to us. For the most part our plan worked well, but one of the most difficult evenings was when we attended a luau. Our two sons were sour-faced, cross-armed, and complaining the whole evening. They sat in stone-cold silence, giving us the fish eye throughout the entertainment, punishing us for making them go.

We had a hard time enjoying ourselves with the negative attitudes of our kids. The complimentary mai tais served as our own personal buffers against the bad vibes of our seemingly ungrateful and grumpy teens. Encased in our frustration was the running sound that swirled through our heads that went something like this: "Ching-ching!" This Hawaiian experience was costing us some significant bucks. We wondered if taking the kids on vacation was worth it. We felt awful and the evening seemed like a total waste.

A few weeks after our return, we were having dinner with Matt's parents and family. They asked about our Hawaii vacation. We started to say what a waste the trip had been, when we overheard the boys talking about how much they enjoyed the trip. They began reminiscing about their favorite evening. They got excited talking about the girl sitting across from Paul and how she made eyes at him, and other stories from the event. What evening was that? You guessed it. They said their *favorite* part of the vacation was the luau. Go figure.

You can never really know for sure if your teen is having a good time or not. And they probably won't let you know. Developmentally this is a time when they need to separate from parents. They just can't say they like what their parents like. They have to be different. Just remember that it's a temporary stage, so hang in there.

In the meantime, you might want to balance out the lists by adding a number eight to your list of "Seven Things a Teenager Will Never Say." Let it read: "I can't wait until our next family trip. I love going on vacations with my parents."

And know and trust that, secretly, they just might.

Dealing with Your Child's Outrageous Emotions

It was the weekend before final exams. Monica wanted to spend the night at her girlfriend's house along with a group of friends. Her mom said that she could join the group for the evening, but that she had to be ready to be picked up by 11 p.m. Sharon told her daughter that she wanted her to get a good night's sleep, so that she wouldn't be tired going into exam week.

At 9:30 p.m. the phone rang. It was Monica asking if she could spend the night.

"Mom, all the other girls get to stay. Why can't I? Please?"

"No. You need to get sleep this weekend so you will be well rested for next week's exams. I will see you at 11." Click.

A few minutes later the phone rang again.

"But Mom, why can't I stay overnight? It's not fair. You are the only mom not letting her daughter spend the night. We'll go to sleep early. I promise."

"Honey, I know that you are disappointed, but your exams are coming up. Have fun with your friends until I pick you up. Bye-bye."

Five minutes later the phone rang again. This time Sharon refused to answer.

At 11:00 Sharon picked up her daughter. On the drive home Monica harangued her mom. She was outraged that her mom was being so unreasonable. Sharon mostly stayed silent while her daughter recited a litany of condemnation:

- "You don't have a good reason for not letting me spend the night."

- "You won't let me have a good time with my friends."

- "You don't respect me."
- "You're a bad parent."
- "You don't trust me to make my own decisions and learn from my mistakes."
- "You're on a power trip, Mom."

Sharon calmly responded, "I can hear how mad you are. There will be other times when you can spend the night. It's late, I'm tired, and you're angry. Let's not discuss this right now. Let's talk tomorrow." Sharon realized the conversation would go nowhere and would probably end up in an argument. So she didn't respond to her daughter's criticisms. She knew it would do no good anyway.

How would you respond?

When your child expresses a charged emotion like resentment, anger, blame, hurt, sadness, or fear, how do you typically respond? If you react, instead of act, you might automatically pull away, get angry, or attempt to use logic or reason to stop these emotions. Some parents immediately step in and make an effort to fix it or smooth things over. Some take on their child's feelings and start acting like an adolescent themselves. Others use punishment to convey disapproval to their adolescent for expressing negative emotions.

Parents who punish negative emotions are frequently unable to cope with these feelings in themselves. When their teen begins to talk back it triggers in them a harsh response that is rooted in their past. We all bring baggage from our past into our role as parents, and it is critical to be aware of and attempt to work through these issues so they don't interfere with the relationship with our kids. In *Parenting from the Inside Out,* Dr. Siegel and Mary Hartzell write:

> Experiences that are not fully processed may
> create unresolved and leftover issues that in-

fluence how we react to our children. These issues can easily get triggered in the parent-child relationship. When this happens our responses toward our children often take the form of strong emotional reactions, impulsive behaviors, distortions in our perceptions, or sensations in our bodies.

When we punish our kids for their strong emotional responses, it sends an unspoken message to stop expressing these normal and very human parts of themselves. An important piece of who they are gets denied and repressed. And our parenting is impaired because we are unable to think clearly and remain flexible.

Jason grumbles to his dad about how much he has to study and how stressed he is from his schoolwork. His father jumps in and tries to fix the problem by demanding that he work harder and spend less time on his cell phone and computer.

Tina responds to her daughter's complaints about feeling fat and ugly by countering her criticisms with compliments. "Honey, you look beautiful just the way you are. Your body is perfect. What are you complaining about?"

These responses don't really work, for you or for your child, so we invite you to try something different.

Something that works far better

Whenever your teenager tries to communicate how he feels, no matter how frustrating, demanding, or difficult it may be for you, simply listen to what he has to say and reflect back the emotions you hear.

That's right, *listen and reflect*. Be receptive to what he has to say. Receptive parents are most effective when they remain calm and connected, as difficult as that can be in the heat of the moment. Parents who listen and reflect make communication safe.

Listening with compassion and acknowledging feelings can profoundly transform a situation beyond our imagination.

Let your daughter experience your presence as a safety container to feel and express whatever emotion comes up. Keep your attention on what she is attempting to say by focusing on her verbal and nonverbal communication, rather than on preparing a response. This allows her to identify and let go of negative, bottled-up emotions. When you identify and label the emotion your daughter is feeling, she feels seen and heard. This will also aid her in developing emotional intelligence.

Conversing with teenagers about their thoughts, feelings, and experiences helps them to know themselves more deeply. It provides them with the essential interpersonal experiences needed for self-understanding and building their social skills. Listening with compassion and acknowledging feelings can profoundly transform a situation beyond our imagination. It can de-escalate arguments and reduce problem behaviors in a family. Research even suggests that releasing pent-up emotions helps prevent physical illness.

What is deep listening?

When we are compassionate listeners we experience a resonance with those to whom we are listening. To witness another person is to be approachable, available, and dependable. Deep listening allows us to be nonjudgmental. Trying to understand another person's position creates an alignment with them, and the two people experience a sense of joining. Being open-minded allows a process to take place that invites an exchange of emotions. Kids need parents to stay clear, centered, and available so that they can fully experience and eventually let go of painful thoughts or emotions.

In his informative book on parenting adolescents, *Yes, Your Teen Is Crazy,* Michael Bradley distinguishes between good and bad listening. He writes:

> Bad listening is interrupting, asserting your power, and inviting a confrontation. It's taking your child's words too seriously, forgetting that being a brain-challenged adolescent means having lots of impulsive, illogical, and provocative thoughts that don't necessarily represent what the kid was trying to say.

Bradley goes on to say that good listening means setting aside your own thoughts and feelings in order to let your adolescent talk. Listen without judgment. It means putting yourself in her shoes, seeing the world from her perspective. It means doing this particularly when you are tired, frustrated, or angry.

When teens know that you will consider their point of view and take them seriously, they are more likely to be open about their problems and feelings. When you respect your teenagers' opinions and listen carefully, they will be able to communicate openly, and develop the inner strength and courage to do the right thing when you are not around.

Practice being a good listener

Rehearse being a good listener, rather than a fixer. If you find yourself having difficulty with listening, then step back for a moment and observe what judgment you might be holding. Sometimes a roadblock to being a deep listener is our own tendency to judge. Judgment separates us from others. Understanding, along with deep listening, reduces anger, bad attitudes, and back talk.

Do not make the mistake of taking personally what your teenagers say. Your role is to listen and to allow them to express their feelings. Jumping in and trying to fix or change the way they feel only disrupts the healing process. It may be valuable to remind yourself that these feelings are not at all about you, but are about their internal struggle to come to know themselves better.

In our opening story, Sharon had to call upon every ounce of self-discipline and willpower not to yell at her daughter. She also knew enough not to punish Monica for her tirade. As difficult as it was for her, Sharon allowed her daughter the space to express her anger and frustration. Eventually, Monica grew weary of her complaining and fell silent. The next day, when the issue was no longer explosive, each shared their feelings from the night before. The issue soon became ancient history, but the connection between mom and daughter was strengthened.

Creating a safe environment for your teen to talk freely and allowing deeper feelings, fears, or tears to emerge is a crucial step toward greater emotional connection, growth, and healing. Deal with your teenagers' outrageous emotions by giving them the profound gift of deep listening.

Parenting Wisdom from
Baseball Legend Yogi Berra

Yogi Berra was one of the best players and most colorful characters in the entire history of major league baseball. Yogi was a star catcher for the New York Yankees for seventeen years from 1946 to 1963, leading them to ten World Series titles. In 1972 this baseball legend was elected into the National Baseball Hall of Fame.

Yogi has a unique relationship to the English language, and a knack for saying things in a different, yet profound way. People quote him all the time, even though one of his most famous "Yogi-isms" is, "I never said most of the things I said."

Believe it or not, we have found that there are important parenting lessons to be mined from Yogi's sayings. He didn't exactly spout off on the subject of parenting, but many of his Yogi-isms can actually be helpful to parents of teenagers. Here are three of Yogi Berra's most famous sayings with applications to parenting teenagers:

1. *"You can observe a lot just by watching."* Teenagers are constantly changing emotionally, mentally, physically, and spiritually. We need to become sensitive to these changes in order to discover who they are becoming, rather than who we want them to be or who we think they are.

No two teenagers are exactly the same, even if they are growing up in the same family. I was challenged by the differences in our three kids. Academic studies came easy to me. Because I was an excellent student when I was in high school, I expected all my kids to get straight A's. As our kids grew and matured, I had to see that this was not to be the case.

This is where this pearl of wisdom from Yogi helped me. I had to learn to see my kids for who they are, rather than who I wanted them to be. After observing, I realized that each child was a different kind of learner. One was super-conscientious about school, another was an incredibly hard worker, and the other was simply not very interested in school at all. I struggled to find the balance between holding up the importance of education and earning good grades on the one hand, and accepting each of our children for their uniqueness on the other.

By paying attention you will not only learn a lot about your changing child but you will also learn a lot about yourself in relationship with your child. You might become aware of your parenting style, how you create and handle conflict, and what you do with your anger. You might even learn how to strengthen the relationship with your parenting partner.

2. *"It ain't over 'til it's over."* These oft-quoted words of wisdom by Yogi remind us that our teenagers are in transition. At sixteen or seventeen or even eighteen years old they are not a finished product but are in the process of becoming their adult selves. They will continue to grow the rest of their lives.

    To help keep your sanity, maintain a consistent attitude of respect and caring, model responsibility, and treat your teenager with love and understanding. They will eventually outgrow the disconcerting and oftentimes frustrating narcissistic behaviors of their teenage years. They will grow up.

    Our oldest son is a sophomore in college. It is astounding how much he has changed and matured in the past two years. He is more thoughtful, more responsible, more respectful and kinder to members of the family than he was in high school. He is insightful and reflective. He has gradually outgrown most of the negative, self-centered teenage behaviors that made us think he would grow up to be an uncaring person. And we know now that he will continue to grow and mature into his adult self in the years to come. What a difference a year or two out of high school makes.

A parent of one of my former senior students wrote the following e-mail to me: "Last school year I almost threw in the towel for my inability to have consistent positive communications with my son. He is now less argumentative, more communicative, more sensitive, and realizes, albeit not fully, that he is not the center of the universe."

When you are frustrated by your teen's lack of maturity, crazy decision-making, irresponsibility, and disrespectful and egotistical behavior, remind yourself that he or she will not always be that way. Talk to friends who have a twenty-something son or daughter. They can give you a sense of perspective. Ask them how their kid has changed. It will restore hope for you. We're relatively certain that they will substantiate Yogi's assertion that, *It ain't over 'til it's over.*

One last note: parents will continue to worry about their children, even when they are adults. So it's really *never* over!

3. *"When you come to a fork in the road, take it."* Many parents are afraid of making the wrong choices when it comes to their kids. We know this from our own experience. We ask ourselves: Is it the right choice? How will it affect my child? What should we do? What actions should we take? We even search out answers from the experts, believing they will know what direction to take.

We think these words of Yogi could become a popular mantra for parents of teenagers, "When you come to a fork in the road, take it." This is because there are constant decisions that must be made while parenting during the teen years. Youth push for independence and sometimes we are not sure what to do. Can I go to the concert? Can I go over Jon's house and then out to a movie? What to do with sassing? How to respond to the f-word? How to handle intense emotions? How to handle the dating scene? What if I discover that my child is sexually active? What if they're using drugs?

Parents, it is important for you, no matter what the situation, to trust your intuition and instincts. Educate yourself, get perspective from those closest to you, or seek out professional help, if needed, then make your own informed decision and act. It's less important if it is the perfect decision; just take some kind of action.

No one has the right answer for your particular situation except you. Make a choice that feels right to you. Then don't look back. Don't dwell on it. Move forward. If you need to make a corrective action, then do so. Learn from your mistakes and make positive changes, rather than second-guessing yourself.

As you model for your family decision making and learning from mistakes, you are teaching your children how to take action during the difficult times. The ability to make good decisions is an important life skill. Let your kids make as many decisions as possible, so they can learn this life lesson early on in their lives.

Keeping a positive attitude

As Yogi Berra knew from his own experience, success in life comes not only from hard work but also from having a positive attitude. We can apply this as well to parenting teens. It is easy to get discouraged and feel like a failure at parenting, especially if our teens are not behaving or thinking like we expect them to. It is tempting to look at our kids' poor decisions and sometimes reckless behavior and blame ourselves for being bad parents. We need to keep things in perspective.

Parents, keep a positive mental attitude. It may help us to recall another of Yogi's sayings, "Ninety percent of the game is half-mental." The next time you feel like you want to quit at the parenting game, find a way to keep a positive understanding of what is going on with your adolescent at this stage. Then step back, take a deep breath, look for ways to take care of yourself, and remember that this too will pass. Find comfort and a bit of offbeat humor in reciting silently to yourself the parenting wisdom of Yogi Berra, "It ain't over 'til it's over. "

Wake-Up Call

For almost a year Joey and his parents came to sessions in my office. He was a fourteen-year-old high school freshman. His parents brought him to therapy because he had a bad attitude, was irritable and angry all the time, and was not working up to his potential in school. Joey's parents insisted that he was capable of doing much better.

Cathy and Joe Sr. wanted me to fix their son. Their expectations were that I would somehow manage to get him more motivated in school and change his bad attitude. They wanted Joey to communicate more respectfully with them and be more involved in the family. They wanted me to "show him the light," the same light that they were unable to get him to see.

The father was disappointed in his son. He described Joey as a mediocre student, quite different from him. Joey's lack of initiative was foreign to him. Both Cathy and Joe Sr. could not comprehend why Joey did not put more time into his studies.

Joey was an only child and a boy of privilege. His parents did not understand his ungrateful attitude and why he was not happy. Throughout his life his parents showered him with opportunities. They believed these experiences would help shape him into a successful young man. Cathy and Joe were proud of all that they provided for their son. He went to the finest educational institutions in the area, had afterschool music and equestrian classes, and had vacation opportunities that other kids only dreamed of. They could not comprehend why he was not appreciative. He had so much more than most kids his age.

The parents worked long hours in the family business in California's Silicon Valley. Hard work and success were important qualities they wanted to instill in their son. Right now, it seemed like they were failing, and, for Joey's parents, failure was not an option.

Revealing the unspoken

In one of our earlier sessions I had the family draw a portrait of the family business, depicting the impact it had on each family member. One person began drawing, and then each family member took turns adding to the picture. Together we explored the artwork. The realization emerged that the boy felt that the business was more important to his parents than he was.

Fortunately, the parents understood fairly quickly how abandoned their son felt. They put a lot of their energy into the business. They had forgotten that their son was just a child. He so often acted more like an adult than a child.

Over time Joey was able to verbalize his anger and resentment regarding the amount of his parents' time the family business consumed.

> Unspoken expectations and built-up resentment are capable of ruining a family.

The parents were able to hear his anger and resentment, and were willing to change. They wanted to stop the erosion of the family and begin to rebuild the damaged relationships. Joey was lucky. Many children are not fortunate enough to have parents so willing to look at their contributions to the breakdown of relationships. Unspoken expectations and built-up resentment are capable of ruining a family.

The father's dream

One afternoon Joe Sr. came to the counseling session alone. He wanted to share a dream he had earlier that week. Sometimes dreams reveal the answers we already know. He entitled it, "The Father's Wake-Up Call":

> It was a cold fall night and I came home from work late again. The day left me feeling

stressed and my mind was still on work as I arrived home. My son was waiting at the back door when I entered the kitchen from the garage. I noticed that I was irritated when I saw him waiting for me. Joey appeared to be about ten years old in the dream.

During our meal, he asked me how much money I made an hour. Bothered by the question I muttered that it was none of his business.

"What makes you ask such a thing?" My question was meant to demean.

"I just wanted to know." Joey's voice was almost inaudible. Eyes cast down. "Please tell me."

To put an end to this ridiculous conversation I told him. "I make $50 an hour, if you really must know." Then he lowered his head and asked if he could borrow ten dollars.

In the dream, I was impetuous and yelled at him for asking for money. Then I demanded that he go to his room. After hearing the door shut, I intentionally raised my tone, complaining to my wife about his selfish request.

Settling into the evening, I found myself feeling a little guilty about my harshness. I entered his bedroom to see if he was awake. Sitting on the side of his bed I apologized for my grumpy behavior and handed him the ten bucks he asked for.

"Oh, thank you, Daddy!" Joey was smiling as he jumped out of bed and lifted the cardboard box hidden under his bed. As he pulled out several crumpled bills, I could feel the anger swelling inside of me again.

> What kids remember are the memories that were created when spending meaning-ful time with family.

As Joey counted his savings, I ordered him to tell me why he would dare ask for more money when he already had money stashed away.

"Because I didn't have enough, but now I do, Daddy. I have $50. Now I can buy an hour of your time."

Remembering what not to forget

The meaning of Joe Sr.'s dream revealed what he already knew but had forgotten. It's time to slow down, step back, and rethink the meaning of important relationships.

It is easy to get caught up in work, in the material world, and in the need to succeed, and forget what really matters most.

Twenty years from now when your children are grown, they will not be reminiscing about how proud they were of your long work hours and all the money you made. What kids remember are the memories that were created when spending meaningful time with family.

And at the end of their lives, most people don't wish that they had put in more time at the office. Like Joey's father, you may wish that you had spent more time with your kids. So take advantage of the moments you have right now. It is never too late to build rapport by spending time with your family and creating special memories.

Finding the Balance

"What do you wish your father would have done differently in parenting you?" Year after year in Steve's senior Marriage and Family class, students' answers to this writing exercise are about the same. The most common response is: "I wish he had spent more time with me." Others include:

- "I wish that my dad had been home more often and not always traveling."

- "I wish that he had spent more time with me, come to more of my volleyball games, been at work less, and at home more."

- "I wish that he had spent more one-on-one time doing things with just him and me."

- "I'm hurt that he was not interested in me and he was too preoccupied with his career."

- "I wish that he had played more sports with me."

- "I wish that he had talked to me more."

Harvest those moments

Teenagers will rarely tell you outright that they want to spend time with you. It often appears like they want just the opposite. Many parents presume that their high schoolers do not want to be with them. So they act on these false assumptions and stop expecting their teens to join in family gatherings or other outings.

All kids, even older teens, need and want time with their parents. While it is true that most teens' first choice would probably be their friends over family, this doesn't mean they don't want to spend time with their parents anymore. They just don't want to do the same things that they did when they were younger. Personal time spent with your child nurtures a promising relationship, and it is the impact of these moments that kids remember most.

What is so difficult about giving children our time?

There are many pulls on a parent's time. There is the pressure to work long hours in order to provide for the family and to achieve career advancement. There is the need to provide for the basic necessities of family life—shopping, preparing meals, cleaning, driving the kids to school, sports, and social activities. There is the spousal relationship that needs care and attention. With all these demands it is not easy balancing time with spouse, friends, hobbies, job, and kids.

Many parents are too busy or distracted to make time for their kids. Job-related stress, depression, unhappiness, and addiction to drugs, alcohol, or the Internet can be easy distractions from family life. Parents tell themselves, "Later. I'll do it later." The truth is: It's later than you think.

Four strategies to help busy parents spend more time with their kids:

1. *Share family meals together.* Make it a priority to eat together often. This can be challenging with busy schedules. There are late nights at the office, practices for the kids, meetings, music lessons, and sports. Despite these obstacles, find a way to share meals as often as possible. Oh, by the way: Leave the TV set off.

You might be interested in knowing about a study done at the Cincinnati Children's Hospital. They found that adolescents who shared dinners with their families five times a week were

> Make it a priority to eat together often.

least likely to experiment with drugs or be depressed, and most likely to excel at school and have a healthy

51

social life. The value and importance of family meals are covered in more detail in the next chapter, pages 55–60.

2. *Make appointments.* If you are working long hours and find it difficult to find time to spend with your kids, we suggest that you set up "appointments" with them. Write them on the calendar. Set up a definite time to get together and be sure to keep your commitment. Your kids need to know that your word is good and that you will keep your promises. This is another way for you to let them know that they are important to you.

Debbie takes her daughter out to lunch every Thursday. She picks her up from school and for half an hour they eat at a local fast-food restaurant. It is a simple action that has a profound impact, and her daughter looks forward to it weekly.

3. *Take an extended trip.* Some of you might be thinking, "Oh yeah, right!" But a trip together is time without the distractions of home. Plan a vacation or take one kid at a time on some of your business travels. Dennis takes his daughter on a backpacking trip every summer. Just the two of them. The tradition began when she was strong enough to carry a backpack. Every summer they both look forward to it. They have a great time spending three days hiking in the wilderness and being with just each other.

4. *Do the things your teen likes to do.* Share activities together that your son or daughter enjoys. When I ask our seventeen-year-old son Paul to go to a movie, he replies, "Nobody goes to the movies with their parents." So instead we go to a San Jose Sharks hockey game or to an Oakland A's baseball game. Our sixteen-year-old daughter, on the other hand, doesn't mind going to the movies with Dad.

Consider the interests of your son or daughter and make time doing what they enjoy. It might be spending an afternoon riding your mountain bikes, going to a basketball game, shopping, hiking, going out for hamburgers, skiing and snowboarding together, attending your daughter's swim meet, working on your teen's car, watching your son play hockey, or just sitting around talking.

Be present to opportunity

An advantage of spending time with your child is that you will be creating an opportunity for conversation to happen. Most parents find that as their teen gets older, he begins to talk less. But spending time together creates the space for conversations. You will no longer need to squeeze information out by having to ask so many questions. Teens do not like to communicate on demand. The right moment has to be there for them to share.

Alex went on his eighth grade trip to Washington, D.C. When asked about the trip he shared very little, in fact nothing. A month later, as the family was watching a video together, there was a scene of the Vietnam Memorial.

"Hey," Alex shot out excitedly. "I saw that when I went on my D.C. trip!" He then proceeded to share about his experience. It was not the best timing because the movie was interrupted, but his parents listened and did not miss the opportunity. Spending time—in this case watching a video together—created the opening for spontaneous sharing.

Although we can be seduced into thinking that our teens don't want to be with us, they definitely value the time we spend together. When we want to be with them, they get the message they are worthwhile. This is because they are worth a while of our time.

53

The gift of a cultivated moment

Although we can be seduced into thinking that our teens don't want to be with us, they definitely value the time we spend together. When we want to be with them, they get the message they are worthwhile. This is because they are worth a while of our time.

Give your kids the gift they truly need—your presence in living life in the moment with them. Find your balance by going back to the future. When you do, you may hear your teen echoing the words of Tom, a graduating senior, who wrote to his father:

> The past eighteen years I have always known that you were there for me. You have proven to me that you value family over everything else. Thank you so much for always supporting me at my basketball games and other sports I play. I could always hear you and it made me feel better. I know how difficult it was for you to balance family life and work, but it has been your masterpiece. You always find time to come to my games even if it is a work night. I always knew if push came to shove, you would be there for me.

So think twice about how you choose to use your time now. Use it wisely and take advantage of the present by enjoying your teen now.

The Dinner Table

It has become a tradition for us to kick off the holiday season by traveling to nearby Berkeley to see a one-act play called *The Long Christmas Dinner*. It is performed and sponsored by our son's godparents, Cass and Marlene Candell, and their friends. The year I met Steve, he was a member of the cast. All the actors volunteer their time, and the monies collected are used to fund a local charitable organization. The Candell family invites friends into their magnificent home and then transform themselves into characters for this moving drama by Thornton Wilder.

Time is telescoped in *The Long Christmas Dinner* so that ninety years of family life flow through the play without interruption. There are no scene changes. It is the same dinner table year after year, from one generation to the next. There is something poignant about the sameness of the things that ultimately matter most to us, the importance of family, togetherness, and tradition.

Now, I know we have said this before, but it needs to be said again and again. Eat together as a family, even if it is "takeout" between homework and soccer practice. Eat together and talk. This is one of the best occasions to spend time with your teen.

Over the past three decades there has been a decline in families eating dinner together regularly. In 2003, only 61 percent of young people ages twelve to seventeen said that they ate dinner with their families at least five nights a week. Sad, isn't it? The number one reason parents give for not eating together as a family is lack of time.

Family meals are important

The positive impact that family mealtime has on families is too significant to ignore. In a research project conducted by Dr. Blake Bowden of Cincinnati Children's Hospital Medical Center, 527 teenagers were studied to determine what family and lifestyle characteristics were related to good mental health and adjustment. Dr. Bowden and his colleagues found that kids who ate dinner with their families at least five times per week (at home or in a fast-food restaurant) were the least likely to take drugs, feel depressed, or get in trouble with the law. This factor was a more definitive indicator than age, gender, or family type when predicting a teen's behavior. In addition, these teens were more likely to do well in school and to have a supportive circle of friends.

Harvard researchers followed a group of sixty-five youth, examining family behaviors. After eight years of field study they found that family dinners were more influential in fostering good adjustment than play, story time, and events with family members. Other research found that even if there was alcoholism in the family, children who had family dinners together were less likely to become alcoholics themselves. Eating dinner together proves to be important for the well-being of the family.

> The positive impact that family mealtime has on families is too significant to ignore.

With such strong evidence in support of family meals, it is unfortunate that only about half of American families eat dinner together most nights. The hectic world in which we live has pressed in on all sides, making us feel that eating on the run, while unpleasant, is a necessity of modern life.

However, it is possible for us to change this trend. With some determination and planning, we can maintain *The Long Christmas Dinner* throughout the year. The most important ingredient is not what's on the table; we can serve a home-cooked meal or pizza. What does make a difference is that we regularly set aside time to sit down to eat together.

Four valuable advantages your teen will gain by regularly sharing family meals follow.

Four encouraging benefits of family mealtime:
1. *A sense of belonging.* Kids need the security of feeling like they are a part of something greater than themselves. Family mealtime nurtures a sense of belonging for teens so that they will have less need to seek acceptance and inclusiveness elsewhere. Sometimes kids seek connection through sexual intimacy or by joining high risk-taking groups.

   Dr. David Elkind, author of *The Hurried Child* and professor of Child Studies at Tufts University, says, "Contrary to popular opinion, most young people engage in sexual activity for psychological rather than hormonal reasons." He goes on to say, "If teens feel secure, loved, and appreciated at home, they are not likely to seek comfort and support outside the home in the form of sexual intimacy."

2. *Connection through communication.* Eating together opens the door to communication and connection with one another. There can be laughter and sharing at the table. Problems can be discussed and maybe even solved. Families identify with each other during this time. Eating together encourages strong relationships within the family.

   Sara returned home from volleyball practice at 5:30 p.m. Tuesday evenings are Dad's turn to cook, and there was a tuna casserole and green salad on the table. Dad opened with a blessing giving thanks to the tuna for sacrificing his life for the family's meal and gratitude to the farm laborers who do back-busting work to bring vegetables to our tables. He said it was important to be grateful for what we take for granted.

This blessing prompted Sara's younger brother, Jamie, to start talking about how dumb he thought it was to thank a fish. Sara laughed because she thought it was kind of ridiculous as well. Mom just rolled her eyes.

Dad wanted to know what was so dumb about it. "Tell me, Jamie, what makes you think it's ridiculous to acknowledge a fish or an animal sacrificing their lives so we can live."

"Dad, sometimes you are so weird."

Mom chuckled and said she agreed, but deep down she appreciated the values of her husband's philosophy. The kids knew this too. Before you knew it the dinner conversation became philosophical and shifted to the meaning and purpose of life.

Family members who practice *real* communication know how to laugh with one another. Humor elicits joy. They are able to talk about their feelings, their own points of view, and express their hopes for the future. Practice real communication at your dinner table.

3. *Better academic performance.* Eating as a family appears to give children an edge in the classroom. Studies show that students who ate dinner four or more times a week as a family performed better in school. This was regardless of whether the child was in a one- or two-parent family, and achievement was not affected by whether or not one parent stayed home with the kids.

   A study by the University of Michigan found that the single strongest predictor of higher achievement scores and fewer behavioral problems in children was more family mealtime. Time eating together as a family was far more powerful than time spent in school, studying, in church, or playing sports.

   Mealtime can provide families with an opportunity to engage in intellectual discussions. It teaches good conversation skills. It provides a healthy situation for parents to initiate discussion on moral issues and share values without lecturing.

4. *Healthier lifestyle.* When families eat together they tend to eat healthier. Teens tend to drink more milk and less soda. They also eat less fatty and fried foods and more fruits and vegetables. They also have a higher intake of dietary fiber, and their diets tend to include other essential vitamins and minerals.

> Mealtime is for family members to converse, and the television is not a family member.

Two simple rules to help you commit to regular family meals

These two rules will help you and your children receive the maximum benefits from mealtime.

Rule 1: Keep the meals simple. The eats do not have to be big and fancy. The focus is on spending time with your family members, not on preparing elaborate meals. You might also invite your kids to be involved. Listen to their meal suggestions. Make eating fun. Studies indicate that kids who are involved with meal planning, preparation, and serving tend to have healthier diets than those who don't.

Rule 2: Turn off the boob tube. Mealtime is for family members to converse, and the television is not a family member. Television can often become a barrier to interpersonal connections. Half of American families have the television on while at the dinner table. Turn off the TV. You can't talk with each other when the attention is going toward the boob tube.

Be a caring and connected family

Mealtime is an opportunity to pass on from one generation to the next long-lasting family traditions and cultural customs. Eating together builds community and allows kids to feel connected to something greater than themselves. As you set the family table in your home, remember the profound significance that mealtime makes in the life of your children. Eat together often and keep alive the tradition of *The Long Christmas Dinner* in your home.

Are These the Reasons
Why Your Teen Is Talking to You Less?

It was early Monday morning when I received the call. Sandy was on the line and she was very concerned. "Patt, I need your help. I don't know what's happening. My son hardly talks to me anymore! We used to share all the time. Now I get little more than a grunt out of him. I don't know what's going on. Do you think that he is trying to hide something from me?"

If this sounds familiar, you are not alone. Many parents report that almost overnight their child changes. Out of the blue, their son is moody, rude, and disrespectful, and they find themselves in continuous conflict with him. He is giving them less information than they want and need, leaving them feeling frustrated, anxious, and angry.

Our kids are changing fast. Testing and pushing the limits are part of a teen's job description. The goal is to move toward independence and they do this by pushing. Often parents are seriously thrown off by the new parenting challenges.

Talking less to parents begins during the early years of adolescence and continues throughout high school. It is normal. Teens need to temporarily move away from mom and dad and seek their independence. This is called *differentiating*. Talking less is a normal component of this transition. Dr. Anthony Wolf, author of *Get Out of My Life but First Will You Drive Me and Cheryl to the Mall*, writes that when a boy reaches adolescence, he goes into his room, shuts the door, cranks up the stereo, and comes out five years later.

Teens are in the process of leaving behind childhood and stepping toward adulthood. If your son or daughter is talking to you less, wants to be alone more, and chooses to spend more time with friends and less time with family—

these behaviors are typical and not necessarily something to worry about.

Other reasons for talking less

Some teens talk less to their parents because when they do share, they are criticized for what they have to say. Christina, a high school junior, recalled:

> I was telling my mom about how I was worried for Ashley because she got drunk at the party, and all of a sudden my mom started yelling at me to stay away from her. She said Ashley was a bad influence on me and that she never liked her anyway. I stopped talking to my mom when she started disapproving of me and my friends and giving me lectures.

If we respond to our teenagers with lectures, criticism, and anger, then kids will talk less. Teens want to know that you are on their side. Yelling and sermons tell them that you are the enemy.

How you respond to your child will let her know if it is okay to share with you. Your reaction sends an unspoken message. Either you are safe to talk to or not. The chances are good that your teen will come to you more often and share if

- you are willing to pay attention without interrupting,
- you keep your emotions in check and not overreact, and
- you listen respectfully and non-judgmentally.

However, this not easy for many parents to do.

Help your teenager feel understood

Instead of lecturing, let your teenagers experience that you are on their side. After listening to her concerns about Ashley, Christina's mom might reflect back to her:

- "You must have felt scared for Ashley's safety."

- "I am proud of you for noticing that Ashley was unsafe at the party and for watching out for her."
- "I can see that you were concerned for Ashley's well-being."

Teens want and need to feel understood. You do not have to agree with what is said; the key is to listen nonjudgmentally. This can be extremely challenging at times, especially when it is a topic you feel strongly about and you are afraid your teen is heading in the wrong direction.

How do you get information?

When your teenager talks to you, do you barrage him with questions? It is second nature to want to gather more information from our kids. Parents ask questions because they want to know what is going on and to be involved, but teens often feel like they are being given the third degree, so they get angry, defensive, or withdrawn.

Asking direct questions of your teenager is probably one of the least effective ways of getting information. Many teens answer with a monosyllabic response or a grunt.

"How was soccer practice?"

"Fine."

"What did you guys do at Mike's house?"

"Nothing."

Some teens perfect the art of mumbling, and then, when we say, "Would you please speak more clearly?" they roll their eyes and express utter disdain and disbelief that we didn't understand them!

> Parents ask questions because they want to know what is going on and to be involved, but teens often feel like they are being given the third degree, so they get angry, defensive, or withdrawn.

Parents do not normally get a lot of information when directly questioning teens. So we suggest that they ask fewer questions and seek other ways of communicating with their kids.

Three ways to initiate communication that connects:

1. *Stop asking so many direct, personal questions.* Mike resented his mother's prying questions. The reason she asked questions was to feel more involved in his life. When she realized that it was offensive to him, she promised that for the following week she would not ask him so many questions, while assuring him that this did not mean she was not interested in him.

> Another strategy for developing parent-teen communication is self-disclosure on the part of the parent. It helps your teen see you as a human being and not just as a parent.

However, Margo did make it clear that there were some questions she had to ask. Where are you going? With whom? What time will you be home? Will there be parents home? These inquiries are necessary. She is still responsible to supervise him. Mike was doubtful that his mom would actually ask fewer questions, but he agreed to her experiment. To Margo's surprise, within two weeks her son began sharing more with her than when she tried asking so many questions.

2. *"Waste" time together.* To stimulate conversations with teenagers, participate in activities that interest them. Spend time going to the movies, shopping, ballgames, snowboarding—you name it. When parents and teens are "hanging out" together, conversations arise spontaneously.

3. *Self-disclosure.* Another strategy for developing parent-teen communication is self-disclosure on the part of the parent. It helps your teen see you as a human being and not just as a parent. Self-disclosure invites self-disclosure.

Over time Joey was able to verbalize his anger and resentment regarding the amount of his parents' time the family business consumed. The parents were able to hear his anger and resentment, and were willing to change. They wanted to stop the erosion of the family and begin to rebuild the damaged relationships. Joey was lucky. Many children are not fortunate enough to have parents so willing to look at their contributions to the breakdown of relationships. Unspoken expectations and built-up resentment are capable of ruining a family.

When parents are willing to share their personal experiences and life stories with their teenagers, the kids are more willing to share with the parents about what is going on in their lives. Some moms and dads are afraid to be honest about their past. They think that sharing about what they did will give permission for their child to do the same. Not true.

We cannot live our teenagers' lives for them, but sharing our personal stories and life lessons that we have learned is helpful to them. Teenagers still need to find out for themselves how to live life. Kids will make their own decisions and work through their own mistakes, but as parents model self-disclosure, teens will begin to feel safe and comfortable sharing what is going on in their lives.

So invite change in your relationship and open the channels of communication. As you make healthy and necessary changes in how you communicate with your teen, your relationship will shift. By acknowledging the normal teenage behaviors, practicing good listening skills, dialoguing and sharing realistically about life's struggles and joys, and making more time together—even if it is "wasting time"—you will be well on your way to building an influential and lasting relationship with your transforming young adult.

If you love something,
set it free.

If it comes back,
it was and always will be yours.

If it never returns,
it was never yours to begin with.

If it just sits in your living room,
messes up your stuff,
eats your food,
uses your phone,
takes your money, and
never behaves as if you actually set it free in the
first place,
you probably gave birth to it.

—*E-mail humor, author unknown*

PART TWO: LIMITS

Having a child makes you no better
a parent than having a piano in your home
makes you a musician.

When Brian was twelve years old, we were just completing the manuscript for our first book, *10 Best Gifts for Your Teen*. The "gifts" were the non-material variety: respect, room, receptivity, responsibility, and so on. Each of the ten gifts was represented by a word beginning with the letter R. We called them the Ten R's.

Late one afternoon, our son was mindlessly slamming the door to the TV cabinet in the family room. Without thinking, he was opening the cabinet and banging it shut, back and forth. Standing nearby, Patt voiced her displeasure, "Brian. Please don't slam the cabinet door."

Thump.

"Brian, stop slamming the door. I just fixed it, and I'm afraid you're going to break it again."

Without breaking eye contact he whacked it again. Thump.

Patt was furious. "Brian! I told you to stop slamming that door. Now stop right now!"

Looking directly at his mom Brian said, "Which one of your Ten R's is going to get me to stop?"

Whoa.

"I'll tell you which ones. Rage! Resentment! Retaliation! Revenge! It's the dark side of parenting and it'll be our next book! Now stop slamming the door."

None of our original Ten R's could keep Brian from banging that cabinet door. What finally got him to stop was Patt's sense of humor and a relationship of caring that motivated him to respect the request. Right after she went off about "rage, resentment, and retaliation" we all started laughing, and in that moment he decided to stop.

We like to retell this true story because it illustrates a very important point. Limits are not about controlling our kids but about teaching self-control. We establish limits not to make sure our kids behave but to keep our teens safe and teach them how to establish their own inner controls. We can influence their behavior but ultimately they have control over what they decide to do or say.

This section on *limits* helps parents to deal with difficult situations by:

1. establishing boundaries and limits,

2. understanding the critical difference between punishment and discipline,

3. and providing parents with the resources to deal with such challenging issues as teen driving, success in school, marijuana use, and teen sexual expression.

Establishing the right limits and consequences can be frustrating at times. It is not always clear what to do. When teenagers do not follow our directives it can intensify the situation and threaten our sanity. More than once we have considered writing that book on the dark side of parenting!

Lessons from the Butterfly

Prior to moving to the San Francisco Bay Area, we lived in Los Osos, a small town in Central California near San Luis Obispo. People called us Los Sasos de Los Osos. We lived on the corner of Los Osos Valley Road and Montana Way. At that time, ours was one of the last homes before entering Montana De Oro State Park which abutted the Pacific Ocean. Across the street from our home was a sandy trail that led over an enormous sand dune to the ocean. Upon reaching the other side you would find yourself exploring an uninhabited beach on the pristine California coastline. The trail begins by winding through a grove of eucalyptus trees. This grove is a resting place for monarch butterflies as they winter along California's northern and central Coast.

Monarchs follow the same migration patterns every year. To protect themselves from the elements during their exhausting trek, thousands of butterflies cluster together on the leaves of eucalyptus trees. Seeing the brilliance of the packed orange wings hanging together from a branch is like experiencing an autumn day in Maine.

Jason, a new father from our neighborhood, often went strolling through the grove on weekends. On this particular Sunday, as he was enjoying the warmth of the sun's rays streaming through the trees, he came upon a limb with a cocoon attached to it.

Spotting a cocoon is not so unusual. Except this one was pulsating with life. It takes about two weeks for a caterpillar to complete its miraculous transformation into an adult butterfly, and this one was ready to release itself. You can tell because the cocoon becomes more transparent, and is now called a chrysalis.

The father learned too late that individual struggles are essential in building the strength needed to survive in the adult world.

Observing the internal struggle to emerge from its chrysalis, the young father decided to help the butterfly. He pulled out his pocket-knife and carefully slit it open to set her free.

Coming forth, the monarch butterfly stretched her crumpled wings. With her wings dried and hardened, the monarch was ready to soar on her first flight. She fluttered and lifted herself a foot off the ground. Then failed. She struggled again to fly, but fell again. The last time she tried, she dropped to the earth and lay motionless.

The butterfly was dead.

It was only later that Jason uncovered the necessity of the monarch's internal struggle. He learned that the inward laboring and striving strengthens the capacity in the wings and body of the monarch so that when it breaks through the chrysalis by its own efforts, it can survive. The father learned too late that individual struggles are essential in building the strength needed to survive in the adult world. His well-intentioned assistance interfered with the normal process of development and contributed to the butterfly's inability to survive in the world.

Many of us do the same thing with our children that Jason did with the butterfly. We try to help our children so they don't have to struggle so hard. We want to make things easier for them and protect them from life's harsher realities. And, inadvertently, we sabotage their personal ability to survive and even thrive on their own.

A parent's struggle

Greg and Rhonda brought their teenage daughter Molly into counseling because she was not performing to her potential in school and because she didn't want to spend much time with the family anymore. They thought that Molly was depressed.

Prior to counseling, Molly's parents had responded to her unacceptable behavior by imposing stern penalties. They took away her computer privileges, including the freedom to instant message her friends. They also took away her cell phone and put her on restriction. They were sure that her poor performance was influenced by her choice of friends and they wanted to protect her from them. They even removed the posters from Molly's bedroom walls, rationalizing that they were a distraction from her studies. These punitive measures did not help Molly to improve; they only served to exacerbate the situation. Rigid rules had taken precedence over the relationship.

Was she depressed? Of course she was. Who wouldn't be with these kinds of insensitive penalties? Molly confided that she felt like she was in prison. And she was.

In our counseling sessions we identified a couple of parenting issues. One was to recognize and accommodate Molly's developmental stage, and the other was to use discipline instead of punishment to encourage her maturation toward independence. Up to now they were unaware of how they were hindering her growth by trying to manipulate her behavior by withdrawing things and friends.

One of our tasks as parents is to help our kids *individuate*, that is, to assist them in breaking away from us in order to become their own person. Trying to control a teen's behavior doesn't do this. Guidance does.

We discussed how Greg and Rhonda could respond in constructive ways to Molly's disconcerting behavior. First of all, they needed to see their daughter as a young woman with very real and human struggles, not as a possession for them to control. They needed to treat her with respect by encouraging healthy communication.

Greg and Rhonda began to build a more bonded relationship with their daughter. They shifted their attention

from specific undesirable behaviors to being more rela-
tional, and set out to get to know their daughter in a different way. They began to encourage Molly to talk openly
about things that were important to her, and they learned to
listen. They avoided criticizing her. They stopped giving her
directions and instead respected what she was thinking and
feeling. Greg and Rhonda gave Molly the time and attention
required to understand her point of view.

Molly's parents began to establish a routine. They restored
her computer and cell phone privileges. They arranged for
individual tutoring, as well as a set time for homework each
evening, free from the distractions of computer use, instant
messaging friends, TV noise, and cell phone calls. The evening routine helped create a home that felt safe and dependable to Molly and she responded positively.

Greg and Rhonda also learned in therapy that it was normal for teens to move away from parents during the later
part of the teen years, so they became more accepting of
Molly's need for privacy and her need to spend more time
with friends and less time with family. At first this was difficult for Greg and Rhonda because they felt that Molly's
distance was a sign of her rejection of them. Surprisingly, as
they gave her more space, Molly actually spent more time
with the family than she had when she was being punished
with severe restrictions. More important, they learned that
children need to be enjoyed and valued, not controlled.

There are still tensions between Molly and her parents,
but with less emphasis on problems and more on the possibilities for enjoying their relationship, both parents and
teen are doing a better job negotiating the turbulence of the
teen years.

**Four lessons parents of adolescents can learn from the
butterfly:**
1. *Care for your teenager without interfering.* As children
   emerge from childhood into adolescence they have a

greater need for independence and privacy. This predictable course is natural yet often difficult and confusing for both parent and teen. Parental supervision begins to shift to being more collaborative. We no longer need to hover over them like we did when they were little. As teens begin to reach out of the family more and begin to build their own lives, it is critical for parents to respect their schedules when making plans that include them.

Parents still need to provide a cocoon of safety—including clarity, support, consistency, guidance, and love—allowing teenagers to explore and learn under parental supervision. As a family goes through new stages of growth, parents need to reevaluate rules and establish new boundaries. This promotes healthy family functioning.

2. *Give adolescents the time and space necessary to grow into adulthood.* Allowing your teenagers their life experiences, as much as possible without intervening, will reinforce responsible behavior.

Understand that learning can be tough at times and do your best not to jump in and rescue your teen, but remember that leadership (and sometimes protection!) is still necessary. The most profound learning takes place when we let our teens experience the consequences of their own choices. Teens will grow and mature as they learn from their mistakes. Parents will be challenged to practice patience and acceptance during this developmental stage because "our agenda" of how we think our teen "should be" will be confronted again and again.

3. *Be available and approachable without being controlling.* It is a myth that adolescents no longer want parents involved in their lives. Spending time with your teenagers and using your observational skills will help you be in tune with all the changes and challenges they are going through. If you really listen with your eyes, ears, and heart, your teens will let you know what they need.

Teenagers need parents to pool resources with them during this stage of development. This is a time when kids need parents a lot. But, they need us to be there for them in a different way. They don't need us to prevent them from making mistakes, but rather to be there to support them when they stumble and fall. Mistakes can be effective opportunities to teach valuable lessons in a meaningful way. Personal growth comes more naturally by allowing teens to accept the consequences of their own choices rather than by using restrictions, lectures, or nagging.

4. *Put relationships before rules.* Our job as parents is to help prepare our teenagers for adulthood. The relationships we build with our kids will prepare them for the real world when they leave home. Family of origin relationships are the most profound bond in a child's life. Experience within the family unit teaches children how to express themselves in all their other relationships.

There is no question that setting limits and establishing rules are essential ingredients for teaching our teenagers to become responsible adults. But it is the relationship we establish with our kids that will form the foundation and motivation for their growth. Rewards and punishments are not the primary motivators for children, relationships are.

When kids feel that we genuinely care about them, it prompts them to learn. This relationship is the driving motivation for our teens to want to follow our guidance, accept direction, and strive to be their best selves.

You might recognize this saying, "I don't care how much you know until I know how much you care." Teenagers need to know that they are genuinely cared about. They need the love and trust of their parents as they grow to know and trust themselves.

Of course, there are never any guarantees in parenting. Young people must and will struggle in order to grow and mature. And just as Jason learned when he released the butterfly before it was ready to emerge, it is important to recognize that the struggle within is a necessary part of a teenager's journey into adulthood.

Rewards and punishments are not the primary motivators for children, relationships are.

The Biggest Mistake Parents Make

The biggest mistake parents make involves punishing their children. That's right. You heard it correctly, punishment.

I know you're thinking, "Why is it a mistake? If we don't punish our children, they will grow up to be spoiled, out-of-control adolescents. How else will we control our children?"

Discipline is preferred over punishment

Knowing the difference between punishment and discipline will significantly shift the way you prepare your children for adulthood. Many people use these two words interchangeably, but they are drastically different, and the outcomes they produce are poles apart.

Discipline teaches accountability. Discipline encourages responsible behavior while developing an internal locus of control. An interior compass guides a child's decision-making process when parents are not around to make decisions for them. Discipline supports a child's growth and is typically fair and reasonable.

Punishment imposes a penalty for an offense that was committed, and its purpose is to inflict emotional or physical pain. The belief is that if it hurts enough, then the kid will not do it again. The unspoken message is that mistakes are not tolerated. Another problem with punishment is that over time it builds resentment, anger, hostility, and a secret desire for revenge. Punishment is about control; discipline teaches self-control.

Common forms of punishment

Three common forms of punishment are corporal punishment, taking away privileges unrelated to the misbehavior, and verbal assaults. We live in a culture that is rooted in the notion that "might makes right." Trends in parenting often mirror the culture.

When our children were younger, a neighbor shared with us her technique to curb her ten-year-old daughter's temper tantrums. This mother recommended spanking with some neutral object—not her hand, of course— and stated

> People are not for hitting under any circumstances. Corporal punishment is violent, and violence against children is unacceptable. Never strike your child.

that the spanking should hurt the child. Her goal was to use physical punishment as a means to control her daughter's exterior behavior. A violent action taken against a child may appear to work in the moment, but it has deeply damaging effects on a child's self worth. People are not for hitting under any circumstances. Corporal punishment is violent, and violence against children is unacceptable. Never strike your child.

"Under the guise of discipline, physical and emotional violence toward children is legitimized and sanctioned," writes Barbara Coloroso in her award-winning book *Kids Are Worth It!* Children who are abused and neglected often turn to drugs and alcohol to self-medicate the internal pain of not being treated respectfully.

Another form of punishment is penalizing the child by taking away something of value that is not necessarily related to the misbehavior. Taking away the computer use, or the car keys, or a Friday evening with friends has nothing to do with disrespecting a parent.

Last winter our daughter invited a friend to go snowboarding with her. We were going up for the day and had to be on the road by 4:30 a.m. The girlfriend was planning to spend the night. On the drive to our home the girl and her mother got into an argument. After a heated exchange, the mother announced, "Because you have been rude and disrespectful to me, you can't go snowboarding with Mikhaila tomorrow."

They never did make it to our house, and when we called to find out where they were, the girl told us that she couldn't go. This was punishment, not discipline, and this mother's actions punished Mikhaila as well.

Other forms of punishment, although not so obvious, are inappropriate expressions of anger, yelling, humiliation, guilt trips, shaming, and belittling. "How can you be so lazy?" "I wish I never had you." "You'll never amount to anything." "You're such a baby." Some parents use hurtful words to manipulate their children into doing what they want or they ask rhetorical questions like "What's the matter with you? What were you thinking?" Never ask a rhetorical question. Such remarks and questions are abusive and seriously harm a child's self-esteem.

Greg, a high school senior, reflected on how he was parented:

> For the most part I feel like all I learned was negative stuff. All I remember hearing from my dad is, "Why do you have such a bad attitude?" "I hope you don't treat your friends like you treat me." "You're a f--- up just like your brother." When he yells at me and belittles me, what I hear is that I'm not good enough. I feel pressure to be different and that I'm not okay as I am.

Why do so many parents use punishment when it damages a child's self-worth and has serious long-term negative effects on kids? Parents who use punishment tend to react, instead of act, in given situations. They are unaware of their emotional reactivity and act impulsively without thinking about the long-term ramifications. How can parents teach self-control when they are unable to exercise self-control? Kids pick up quickly the unspoken hypocrisy, "Do as I say, not as I do." You cannot teach a behavior if you are not modeling the behavior.

Mary was angry when she caught her son, a freshman in high school, viewing a porn site online. She scolded him and told him he was grounded. He had to stay in his room after school for a week without the use of the computer. He was also forbidden to talk with friends and was not allowed to practice with his school's basketball team. This was followed by a shaming lecture on how bad he was and how she had taught him better than that!

Discipline is teaching

Discipline comes from the Latin word *discipulus*, which means "student" or "learner." Our kids are our students, and it is our duty to teach them self-discipline, responsibility, and the ability to make good decisions for themselves when we are not around.

When Mary caught her son visiting pornographic sites it was a pivotal opportunity to coach him instead of shaming and belittling him. Had Mary placed her attention on her son's emotional life she might not have felt compelled to "fix" or "change" him by demanding him to stay away from pornography. She would have remained calm. When you are in tune with your kid, you talk to him in a way he can hear while talking about your own feelings.

Reflecting on the situation, Mary realized that she had overreacted, and she transitioned from punishment to discipline. Mary began talking with her son about human sexuality. She shared a story about her own brother who got caught by his mother looking in the bra section of a Penney's catalog. This helped normalize the situation. She talked about how desirable and beautiful sex is because we are sexual beings, but when taken out of a sacred context, it can be damaging to relationships.

Mary found that her son listened as she spoke with concern about the possible damaging effects of pornography.

Pornography can be particularly damaging to male adolescents. Establishing self-control is a core developmental task for teenagers. Looking at porn postpones the attainment of this ability. Young males get turned on more quickly by visuals. Looking at sexual pictures can quickly release hormones that produce powerful feelings of arousal. Practicing self-control while sexually aroused is extremely difficult.

Pornography can also be addicting. Its purpose is to arouse. It can feel so good that people don't want to stay away from it. It can encourage unhealthy sexual activity and attitudes. Porn can influence males to see women as sexual objects instead of as real persons. In relationships women are to be respected, loved, and cherished. Porn can interfere with developing healthy relationships with loving interactions. It can negatively influence people and relationships.

Mary took the time to share all of this in her own style with her maturing son. She didn't make a big deal out of natural tendencies to explore the "forbidden." There are no guarantees that he will not visit porn sites in the future, but what really matters is that etched in his mind are the words of his mother. And the next time there is a temptation, he will hear her words and that will influence the choice he makes.

Learning from consequences

Discipline is nonviolent and is centered in principles that teach a child to develop an inner sense of self-control. Discipline is respectful and keeps the dignity of our kids intact. Discipline teaches by applying consequences that are related to the misbehavior or that suggest a positive behavior. When kids are disciplined, they generally do not feel resentful or revengeful because they know that the consequences are fair.

Our friend's fifteen-year-old son was visiting his grandma on her fifty-acre ranch in northern Montana. Without her knowledge, Andrew decided to take his grandmother's pickup truck for a joy ride around the property. Out in the field, Andrew rolled the truck, causing significant damage to the vehicle. Fortunately his injuries were minor. Instead of grounding Andrew for the summer, Grandma and Andrew's parents collaborated and decided to have him work on the ranch—bailing hay, feeding the animals, and repairing fences—in order to earn the money to help pay for the damages he caused. The consequences were related to and appropriate for the "crime" committed. The adults in Andrew's life used this event to teach him an important life lesson about accountability. They didn't yell, shame, or lecture him on how irresponsible he was. They took action that might shape the choices he makes in the future. The statement they made was, "You goofed and you need to make good."

Discipline teaches teenagers to be responsible without robbing them of their self-respect and value as persons.

Discipline teaches teenagers to be responsible without robbing them of their self-respect and value as persons. Rather than trying to control their behavior, use discipline to teach your kids accountability and self-control. You have the choice to empower your children or control them, the choice to discipline or to punish. What choice will you make?

How to Reduce Conflict
Between You and Your Teen

As a senior in high school, Brendan wanted a car. Not just any car. He wanted to buy his friend's 1986 BMW, and he wanted to buy it now. He asked his parents if he could use some of the money that was set aside for his college education to get the car. They emphatically refused his request. "That money is for college. When you get a job and start earning money, then you can buy a car."

Brendan was angry. "Why can't we buy the car now? You know that I am going to get a job this summer."

"When you start working, we'll get the car."

Brendan played the sympathy card, "But I've applied to some places, and no one has called me back. I have no control over that. Let me get the car now."

"Get a job first, and then we'll buy the car."

Brendan stormed off slamming the door behind him.

Conflict between parent and child is inevitable, especially during the adolescent years. When we come home from a busy day at work, the last thing we want to experience is tension or a power struggle with our teenager. However, the very nature of adolescence involves combat. They are fighting for their lives. Their developmental task is to become separate from us. The journey of an adolescent is to discover who he is and how to be self-sufficient. Conflicts help him to define his strengths and recognize his limitations.

Teenagers grow by being in opposition to us. And we grow as parents. Conflict with our adolescents strengthens our nerves and sharpens our parenting skills. If handled constructively, conflict produces positive changes, leads to unity, and promotes collaboration.

Some parents fear conflict with their adolescent, not fully understanding its importance. During the transition from childhood to adulthood, as our teens are coming of age, their search for independence becomes heroic. Teenagers have to step out of their safe and familiar worlds and into the unknown, and for most parents there is great fear around these transitions and changes.

If handled constructively, conflict produces positive changes, leads to unity, and promotes collaboration.

Parents who dodge issues and do not address conflict will not create harmony in their homes, or in their relationships. This is a common mistake some parents make. Avoidance of emotions does not create inner peace or teach children how to regulate inner feelings. Openly communicating about feelings, resolving tensions, problems, and disagreements—instead of submissively withdrawing or letting things slide—builds the skills teens need to deal with the challenges of life.

To handle conflict, parents need to work with the tensions and challenges. Addressing rather than suppressing conflict opens the lines of communication. It gets parent and teen talking to each other, instead of about each other. Conflict that is positively addressed teaches our teenagers how to work harmoniously, coming up with solutions that benefit both parent and child.

Difficult issues involving uncomfortable feelings arise in all relationships. Conflicts with teenagers are inevitable, and often lead to anger, hurt, and blame. In the parent-teen relationship, resolving conflict brings you to deeper levels of understanding. This is a win-win. Understanding and compassion help create a peace-filled home. Remember, ill feelings only become destructive if you persist in not dealing with them or deal with them inappropriately.

Three categories of teen-parent conflicts

Conflicts that we experience with our teenagers can be divided into three general categories. Conflicts arise from:

- developmental issues,
- issues that are primarily the teen's responsibility, or
- issues where the parent has a problem with the teen's behavior.

We will discuss specific strategies to help you reduce the conflict with your adolescent in each of these three areas. Depending upon the category, these conflict issues need to be dealt with differently.

Conflicts rooted in developmental issues:

"Adolescence is a kind of emotional seasickness. Both are funny, but only in retrospect," observes Arthur Koestler. Developmental issues that contribute to conflict between parent and teen include: self-centeredness, moodiness, failure to communicate, the teen taking things for granted, a sense of entitlement, being critical of parents, questioning parents' authority, and the need to develop independence. The following strategies are suggestions for dealing with these developmental issues.

1. *Let go of the need to control.* We cannot change another person; parenting is not about control but about teaching kids to be able to develop self-control. Our role as parents is to set the limits, ground rules, and guidelines; it is not our job to make sure they obey.

2. *Remind yourself that this is normal developmental behavior.* Familiarize yourself with normal teenage developmental behavior, and try not to give in to the behavior nor punish your teen for it. On our family vacation to Hawaii a few years ago, one of our kids said to us, "Why did you waste all that money on a trip to Hawaii? You should have given me the money you spent on my plane fare so that I could buy a new computer." He was engaging in typical teenage egocentric behavior, so we didn't discipline him for his observation, nor did we buy him a computer!

3. *Remind yourself that, in time, this behavior will pass.* There is good news and bad news about adolescent development. The good news is that just like the terrible twos, this stage will eventually pass, and our kids will outgrow these behaviors that often drive us nuts. The bad news is that it may take eight to ten years. A young person is emancipated when she is "paying her own bills." Autonomy may not happen until she is well into her twenties. So in the meantime:

4. *Practice chanting the following mantra: "This is not about me."* When teens do display these disconcerting developmental behaviors, we need to remember that in most cases there is nothing that we have done to cause the anger or moodiness or lack of communication, and often there is little we can do about it. In most cases the behavior has nothing to do with us. Yet we often take it personally. Della went to hug her thirteen-year-old daughter and she withdrew and didn't let her mom touch her. Della felt hurt and carried the feeling all day. So when this happens to you, just repeat silently to yourself, "This is not about me."

One day I was driving Mikhaila to swim practice and she was in a particularly sour mood. I asked her about her time in the 100 meter breaststroke and she snapped at me and made some sarcastic remark.

I said silently to myself, "This is not about me." But I guess I wasn't silent enough.

"What did you say, Dad?"

I borrowed a monosyllabic response from the teenager's handbook: "Nothing."

Conflict situations that are primarily the teen's responsibility:

Poor study habits, procrastination with schoolwork, choice of friends, filling out college applications, getting up and being on time when the carpool leaves, getting a traffic ticket, and losing an item of clothing are a few examples of situations where parents might initiate a quarrel. They are the teen's responsibility, but the parent sometimes will not let go. Here are three strategies to deal with conflicts that arise from issues that are primarily the teen's responsibility:

1. *Avoid the tendency to rescue.* Some parents jump in to rescue their teens. When my son tells me that he is overwhelmed with schoolwork or that he did poorly on a pre-calculus test, I want to jump in and rescue him, instead of supporting him in finding a solution to deal with his problem.

   Rescuing is allowing your daughter to stay home from school to do a term paper, which she had procrastinated about doing, and telling the school that she is sick. A way to hold your teen accountable is to say, "You can stay home, but I'm not calling in sick for you again. I have done it once and I won't do it again. You will have to deal with whatever the school's consequence is for cutting a day of school."

2. *Hold your teen accountable.* A father told us that twice his son called him late at night when he had run out of gas, and twice the dad drove to where he was stranded and helped fill the tank. The third time his son ran out of gas, his dad said, "I'm not coming to get you. You will have to solve this problem on your own." And he hung up the phone. This was very difficult, but the father knew that his son would not learn unless he was held accountable for his poor planning.

3. *Help teens problem solve.* Teens need to learn to cope with adversity, deal with their mistakes, and handle problems. This involves skills that do not come naturally to many people but can be learned. Some teens sabotage themselves with negative thoughts and attitudes. Help them redirect uncomfortable emotions and destructive self-talk into positive outcomes. Teens need to learn to

handle their problems, and may not know how to do this at first without parental guidance. Assist your teenager to identify the problem she is facing, brainstorm creative options to best solve it, and then choose a positive solution to implement. And don't be surprised if she doesn't learn this the first time!

Conflicts that involve parents taking issue with the teen's behavior:

Not getting chores done or picking up after him or herself, teasing or picking on younger siblings, rudeness and disrespect to parents, coming home after curfew, excessive phone or computer use, drinking, smoking, and using marijuana or other drugs are some examples where tension and conflict can arise.

Use these three C's of positive discipline—clarity, consistency, and caring—to teach and guide your teen when faced with any of the situations above.

1. *Clarity.* Inform your teenager that his behavior is disconcerting and how it is upsetting and worrisome to you. This isn't about imposing consequences, which may come later, but about expressing your feelings. Use "I" statements. Examples include:

   - "I am frustrated when I see your bath towel on the floor of your bedroom and not on the rack or in the hamper. I want you to pick up after yourself."

   - "I'm so sad when I hear you teasing your brother and calling him names. It is so hurtful. I want you to stop it right now."

   - "It's not good for you to sit at the computer all day and play games. I'm concerned about your back and neck. It is important for you to balance your computer use with other activities."

Sometimes this will be enough and the behavior will stop. More likely, you will need to repeat yourself many times.

2. *Consistency.* Many parents struggle with being consistent in applying and following through with appropriate consequences. The teen comes home after curfew, and parents shout and holler, "You are grounded for a month." Three days later, the parents let her off restriction. Lack of consistency leads to confusion. A high school junior reported that her mom would yell at her one day for being on the phone too long, and the next day her mom wouldn't mind. It depended upon her mood.

Consistency is easier when the consequences are short. The impact is still as effective. When your teen comes home past curfew on Friday evening, consider grounding him for Saturday evening rather than for the next three weekends. One Saturday evening feels like three weeks worth of restrictions to a teen. Save the longer consequences for more serious issues, such as drinking or drug use.

3. *Caring.* A caring approach looks upon misbehaviors as opportunities to teach and guide your teenager. When parents are locked into the "my way or the highway" thinking, they shut down important avenues of collaborative and open communication with their teen. Teens are left feeling unsupported and end up angry, frustrated, and isolated from parents, and this can create a whole new set of problems.

When conflict is confronted but not resolved

Many times the conflict is not neatly resolved, and parent and teen are left with mixed feelings and anything but a harmonious experience. Let's return to the story of Brendan and the BMW.

Later that evening, after he had calmed down, Brendan sought out his dad. "I know you want me to start working and earning money before I get the car, but it's really frustrating because I have applied for jobs at a lot of places, and I have to wait until I hear from them."

"You're feeling a bit helpless. Like it's out of your control?"

"Yeah."

"Why not fill out a few more job applications. The more you have out there, the more likely you are to find something."

"I just want the car now."

"I know you do, son. It's hard to be patient when you really want something."

The issue was not resolved, and there were still uncomfortable feelings and a difference in perception. But both parents and teen had done their best to deal with this challenging situation.

Skate as if the music were still playing

Parents are challenged to exercise both firmness and compassion in raising children. Sometimes it is best to ignore the rude comment or the misbehavior. Other times it is important that we respond firmly.

While watching the pair's figure skating competition on television recently, we were reminded of the Winter Olympics held in Squaw Valley, California, in 1960. It was the medals round and the Canadians, Barbara Wagner and Robert Paul, were one minute into their program when a small skip in the vinyl record threw them ever so slightly out of step. Instead of panicking, giving up, throwing up their hands in frustration, or resorting to blame, this couple calmly stopped, approached the judges, and asked to begin their program again. They were permitted to start over and they performed flawlessly, as if the music never stopped.

> Keep in mind that music is the underlying rhythm of love. You want to skate with it even when it skips a beat.

In our parenting, how many times have we been thrown off by the unexpected? An angry outburst, foul language, distrustful behavior, a son who comes in past curfew, a daughter not caring about her grades, or maybe even an unexpected pregnancy.

Like the Canadian skaters, we are also invited to learn and grow from the unexpected challenges of life. When your child's behavior throws you off, I wonder what difference it would make if you skated with the challenge rather than entering into conflict. Deeper wisdom emerges when we are able to move through the challenges instead of ignoring the problem or creating more drama.

Assess the tension that exists with your child. Identify who owns the problem. Choose communication and connection with your teenager over devastation and destruction. Keep in mind that music is the underlying rhythm of love. You want to skate with it even when it skips a beat.

By the way, Wagner and Paul became the first pairs figure skaters from North America to win the gold!

Instilling an Attitude of Success

Loving and concerned parents want the best for their children. Sometimes, though, even well-intentioned adults are unaware of what it takes to raise moral and responsible people who contribute to society and who have the strength to make good decisions in life.

Thomas Lickona, professor, lecturer, and author, is a key figure in the character development movement in the United States. He cites several frightening tendencies among today's youth. His findings are cause for deep concern. According to Lickona, youth trends include:

- an increase in dishonesty, lying, cheating, and stealing,

- a growing disrespect for authority figures, including parents and teachers, and

- a rise in self-destructive behaviors, such as self-mutilation, premature sexual activity, substance abuse, and suicide.

If these are the tendencies of our youth, then we adults need to find ways to stem the tide of this behavior that Lickona refers to as a "growing moral decay." What can we do to help develop in our young people the ability to make sound moral choices? What do our kids need from us, the adults in their lives, to grow into responsible and respectful people? Love by itself is not enough.

The Search Institute of Minneapolis, Minnesota has been studying teenager behavior for more than a decade. Troubled by the destructive trends of our youth, they set out to identify what specific experiences, skills, and values youth need to grow into healthy and happy adults. They were able to identify twenty internal and twenty external resources that are critical constructs for healthy development.

The Search Institute identified "40 Developmental Assets" that have a profound influence on shaping teenagers' ability to be moral and responsible adults who contribute to society and who have the strength to make good decisions throughout life. Using a survey entitled *Profiles of Student Life: Attitudes and Behaviors,* nearly one hundred thousand adolescents in cities across America were surveyed during the 1996–97 school year.

> The Search Institute identified "40 Developmental Assets" that have a profound influence on shaping teenagers' ability to be moral and responsible adults who contribute to society and who have the strength to make good decisions throughout life.

The results of this survey are too significant to ignore. They found that the developmental assets—like positive family communication, parent involvement in schooling, and clear boundaries at home, school, and in the community—are pivotal to children's futures and have an enormous influence on their well-being. Consistently, youth who had more of the developmental assets were least likely to engage in four different patterns of high-risk behavior: problem alcohol use, illicit drug use, sexual activity, and violence. In addition to protecting kids from harmful behaviors, having more assets increases the chances that they will cultivate positive attitudes that impact their behaviors, such as earning good grades in school and being able to delay gratification.

When youth are listened to, respected, and appreciated, when they are given solid guidance and clear direction from the adults in their lives, they develop an attitude of success. In order to grow up as healthy and productive adults, teens need to be valued and supported by family, friends, and community. All adults need to step up to the challenge and get involved to help teens develop these essential assets.

Seven interactions to help instill an attitude of success in children:

1. *Endorse healthy dialogues.* Parents who encourage emotional dialogues are equipping their children with life skills to cope with their conflicts and concerns, and get their needs met. All areas of a child's life, from self-respect to decision-making, are impacted by the experiences gained from poignant conversations. Healthy dialoguing teaches critical listening skills and develops the capacity to be empathic and compassionate to the needs of others. Everyone wins with healthy dialogue.

One very simple yet profound way to model and encourage healthy dialoging is by real listening, not pseudo listening. Pseudo listening refers to half-listening or pretending to listen, while allowing distractions to interfere with fully attending to what our kids are saying. Real listening is active listening.

Real listening tells our kids that we are trying to understand and to learn about them. In other words, we love and value them as whole and complete individuals. When we truly listen to our kids, they feel more secure, loved, and appreciated. Why? Because we send the message that we care about them, how they feel, and what they have to say. When we do more listening than talking we are able to talk with our children instead of at them.

If you really listen, your kids will let you know what they need. Express empathy. Compassion, caring, collaborative and nonjudgmental attitudes need to be expressed with words like:

- "How hurtful. . . ."
- "What a horrible ordeal."
- "It's not easy talking about. . . ."

Then paraphrase what you heard your teenager say. Begin a healthy dialogue by first checking out what you heard using the following prompts:

- "So what I hear you telling me is. . . ."
- "I'm not sure I fully understand. Are you saying. . . ."
- "It sounds to me as if. . . ."

These statements invite dialogue. You are restating what you heard and asking for clarification. Your comments will open up communication rather than shutting it down.

Next describe the behavior you are seeing and experiencing without making an accusation. Label the feelings in your teen by commenting:

- "It seems to me that you are angry. I want to understand. Tell me about that. . . ."
- "Is it possible that you might be feeling. . . ."
- "I sense that we might have caused you to feel. . . ."

Show interest in your teenager by facing her, making eye contact, and giving her your full attention. Let her know you are listening by your nodding gestures, facial expressions, or voice tones, like *uh huh.*

Your intentions matter more than your gestures. Real listeners are genuinely interested in trying to understand the other person. They want to learn something about that person, and they want to give help and comfort.

2. *Encourage your kids to get involved in community service.* When we help others it makes us feel good. We feel proud of ourselves when we reach out and give. Service develops character and reinforces positive values. When we touch the lives of those who are less fortunate, we learn life lessons that cannot be taught in a classroom.

Many schools have service requirements. Our sons had a requirement of completing seventy-five hours of community service during their four years of high school. Our daughter's school requires service hours as well. She worked at Sacred Heart Community Services, which distributes food and clothing to needy families. She not only enjoyed doing the service work, she also gained a sense of satisfaction and personal pride in being involved in the program. It made her heart and soul feel good.

Service work does not have to be an individual involvement. Whole families can participate in service projects. One of the best experiences that we shared as a family was when we traveled to Tijuana, Mexico to join with Amore Ministries to build a home for a needy family. We returned from our experience with a heightened awareness of the living conditions of many poor people, a greater appreciation for what we have that we so often take for granted, and a sense of satisfaction that we had done something worthwhile for the family that we served.

3. *Call neighborhood kids by name.* Learn the names of the children and teenagers who live in your neighborhood. Greet them by name when you see them. We have been intentionally reaching out to the kids in our neighborhood, and when we greet them they seem surprised at the gesture. It appears that very few adults do this anymore.

4. *Notice misbehavior and comment on it.* When you see kids in public misbehaving, speak up. Say something. When our neighbor Larry would see grade school kids pick up rocks from people's yard and throw them, he would say something. He was polite but firm in asking them to stop. He would also ask their names and say hi the next time he saw them. He reached out. He knew all the kids and where they lived. It made our neighborhood safer. People today don't often step up and say anything when

they see kids acting out of bounds or misbehaving. It's important that we do so.

When our son was captain of his school's volleyball team, I was attending a game at the competitor's school. A group of students sitting behind me began using foul language. I turned around and said, "Hey guys, there are lots of little children around. Would you please not cuss?" Initially, I was somewhat hesitant to do so, because I was a visitor in their gym, and I didn't know how the students would respond. Thankfully, they apologized for their language and moved to another seat.

5. *Give family members household responsibilities.* Being responsible for household chores plays an important role in your child's development. Duties around the house teach kids that everyone in a family has an important function in maintaining the family. Chores teach youth necessary skills for independent living, like cleaning, laundry, and meal preparation. They also help children develop a basic work ethic of responsibility and reliability. These habits cross over into other areas of their lives, such as school, sports, and work.

> The challenge of parenting is to be the kind of individual you want your child to become.

6. *Be an adult role model.* In the survey conducted by the Search Institute, only one in four respondents said that they see "parent(s) and other adults modeling positive, responsible behavior." Young people do not feel that they have positive adult role models in their lives! This is very sad. We are being challenged to live consciously and model respectful behaviors. All of our words and actions give either a positive or negative message. We are being challenged to be models of respect, caring, consistency, and responsibility. The challenge of parenting is to be the kind of individual you want your child to become.

7. *Teach appreciation of cultural diversity.* Set an example for your kids of being respectful of people from different ethnic groups, cultures, races, and religions. Nonjudgmental attitudes reduce bigotry, prejudice, and hatred. Never tell racist jokes or make comments that encourage racial stereotypes. We can help our kids to develop tolerance by: modeling for them a genuine respect for persons of different cultures and races; speaking respectfully about people of other races, religions, and ethnicities; exposing our kids to people of different cultures and races; and by challenging racial stereotypes and racist language.

These are only a few of the many ways that we can instill an attitude of success in our children. Let's take care of the future leaders of our country by giving them what they need to thrive in life. Parents alone cannot do this job; it will take all of us. The Search Institute writes:

> Everyone—parents and guardians, grandparents, teachers, coaches, friends, youth workers, employers, youth, and others—can build assets. It doesn't necessarily take a lot of money. But it can make a tremendous difference in raising confident, caring young people. What it takes is building relationships, spending time together, and being intentional about nurturing positive values and commitments.

Instilling an attitude of success in our children does indeed take a village. Working together, we can make a profound difference in the lives of our children and in the world in which we live.

Parenting on the Edge

We receive many e-mails from distraught and confused parents seeking counsel. Here is a sample:

- My twelve-year-old daughter is always telling me to "shush" or is embarrassed when I talk. She is rude and responds to me in a nasty way. How do I respond?

- My son was IM-ing a friend and I started reading his message. He had a meltdown and yelled, "Why can't you trust me?" I think I have a right to know who he is talking to and what they are writing. What do you think?

- Our teen boys are constantly fighting and putting each other down. We need help!

Teenagers have attitude. Barbara and Dennis Rainey, authors of *Parenting Today's Adolescent* and parents of four teenagers, write:

> At the very core of adolescent behaviors is pride, rebellion and undisguised self-centeredness. It is the root disease of the human heart. Because teens are trying to figure out who they are, what they are supposed to do, what's expected of them, all of these issues focus on the big *me*.

Teens need the limits that parent can provide in order to temper this self-centered behavior. Young people could be headed for certain trouble if they stay focused on self. Limits provide a cocoon of safety for teens, a structure in which they can grow toward the maturity of adulthood.

Families need rules in order to function. Kids need limits to feel safe, secure, and loved. But as they grow into adulthood they begin pushing against them. Expect that. Testing the limits is part of growing up. Teens want to prove to you,

and themselves, that they are independent from you and are ready for
more personal responsibility. This is
a healthy process. In each of the situations above, the kids are pushing
the limits and testing authority.

While parenting a teenager we have to continually reevaluate the limits we set.

Why is it difficult drawing the line when teens push beyond our comfort zone? Some parents don't want their kids to be mad at them. They need to be liked. They want to be the "cool parent."

It is also tricky to draw the line because our teenagers are changing so quickly emotionally, physically, and mentally. It is almost as if we are running to catch up with them, like we are on the edge. We can become overwhelmed, some-times paralyzed and unable to act. We may be thrown off by their changes and unsure of what limits to set. Is it okay for my daughter to "shush" me? Do I impose an ultimatum when my sons fight? What do I do when my preteen blocks the computer screen from me?

Adapting with each developmental change

While parenting a teenager we have to continually reevaluate the limits we set. Adapting to the mental and emotional changes kids go through challenges parents to be flexible. Often teenagers will push the limits when the limits are outdated and need revising. Kids challenge when change is needed.

When our daughter turned sixteen, she asked us if she could get her belly button pierced. Steve carried the belief that only rebellious, lost kids get body piercings, and that it would be absolutely out of the question for her to get one "as long as she lived under our roof." But after some push-ing and prodding he was open to discussing it. He shared his reservations with Mikhaila and she listened. Then she shared her viewpoint and one after the other she addressed his concerns. He listened. They both felt good about the dialogue and it continued until there was some compromise.

One of Steve's greatest concerns was that there might be health risks involved. They decided to consult with Mikhaila's pediatrician and discuss the issue. To Steve's surprise Dr. Vora said that the piercing did not present any significant health risks. Steve had been hoping that the doctor would help convince Mikhaila that it was a bad idea. But the information Dr. Vora shared didn't support Steve's objections.

Mikhaila is a responsible daughter, an excellent student, and a dedicated member of her swim team. Piercing her belly button would not turn her into a lazy, rebellious teenager. In the end we gave her permission to have the piercing. Never in a million years would Steve have thought that his teenage daughter would have a pierced belly button, but he was willing to be flexible and adaptable.

Permissive parenting

There are two common mistakes parents make with limit-setting, and they are at opposite ends of the spectrum: becoming too permissive or becoming overly strict. Both are the result of poor parental boundaries and are often a manifestation of the parent needing to be liked.

Overindulgence—giving kids too much and demanding too little from them—is a common phenomenon in the new millennium. Parents want their kids to be happy, and they have a misinformed belief that happiness comes from having a perfect life, devoid of any hardship or pain. This approach does a great disservice to children. One father told me that he gives his son a great deal because when he was a kid he didn't have much. "I want to give him opportunities to discover life with resources I never had." Even his son admits he is spoiled.

Research is uncovering the harmful effects of permissive parenting. Dan Kindlon, a professor of psychology at Harvard University, conducted a study entitled "Parenting

Practices at the Millennium," in which he surveyed more than 1,000 parents and 654 students in "advantaged" families across the country. Kindlon found that parents earning more than $100,000 a year were more likely to rate their child as spoiled. These parents also demonstrated more permissive attitudes about drug and alcohol use by their kids than parents with lower incomes.

Permissive parenting, that is, parenting with too few limits, creates anxious, unhappy, and self-centered kids. It also puts teens at risk for a host of problems, including eating disorders, underachievement, and unregulated attitudes about sex. In his study, Dr. Kindlon found that girls who reported that they were "very spoiled" were three times more likely to have driven drunk and two times more likely to have smoked marijuana in the last month. Boys who rated themselves as spoiled were at higher risk for drunk driving, lying, cheating, and skipping school.

Rigid parenting

On the other hand, what happens when limit-setting is overly strict? Teenagers whose parents maintain tight reigns on them in high school tend to go wild when they get to college and are free of parental restrictions. They have not had opportunities to develop an inner locus of control because mom or dad had all the control. When the external restrictions are no longer in place, kids are unable to exercise the internal constraints necessary to make good decisions. So they go out when they should be sleeping and drink or do drugs when they should be studying. Many of these kids earn very poor grades during freshman year, and some even flunk out of school.

Kids learn how to handle freedom when they are given more and more personal responsibility as they get older, while still under the supervision of mom and dad. By senior year a reasonably dependable teen is able to make most decisions with only peripheral guidance from parents. That is because she has had lots of practice making choices through-out her high school years.

Limit-setting guidelines:

1. *Know what to expect.* Do not be shaken when your teen-ager gets surly. Because of the challenging nature of adolescence, parents may find it easy to think the worst about their kid. Teens are working toward being free from reliance on parents both psychologically and mate-rially. This is an important developmental task they need to accomplish. Conflict typically increases during this period mostly because the teen brain is not a finished product. Some of the normal developmental changes you can expect from your teen are:

   - mood swings with emotional highs and lows,
   - wanting to spend less time with the family and more time with friends,
   - challenging the rules and pushing the limits, and
   - self-centered behaviors.

   Knowledge can help you to keep your cool during stress-ful situations.

   For the mother who is being "shushed" by her twelve-year-old daughter, realize that this is a fairly normal behavior of early adolescence, so be patient with her. You might say to her, "I'm offended that you tell me to shush. It is rude. You can say to me that you don't want to talk right now, but don't just tell me to shush." You don't want to pester your teen about every little thing she does or doesn't do. Pick and choose what issues really matter most.

   When a child is ten it may be appropriate for parents to closely monitor their child's computer use, and to insist on knowing who she is communicating with via Instant Messaging. But by the time they are in their teens they begin to need their privacy. It is not appropriate to read their IM dialogues, to listen in on their phone conversations, or to read their journals. Parents who do this are exercising poor boundaries.

> Adapt your parenting strategies or expectations to eliminate unnecessary conflict.

Our daughter often covers the computer screen when we pass by, even though she knows our eyes are so bad we can't even read it without our specs! She is not hiding bad language or covering up things she shouldn't be writing. She simply feels an intense need to guard her privacy.

Teens require and deserve their privacy, and parents need to both understand and respect this. The only exception to this general rule is when a teenager is engaging in risky behaviors, such as drug or alcohol use, teen sex, or sexually explicit conversations online. Then we must intervene to care for her safety through closer supervision and observation.

2. *Remind yourself that conflict is predictable.* When parents set limits, conflict may follow. When setting limits, do not get pulled into a control battle with your teenager. Manage your feelings so that you do not get out of control. Don't use consequences as a threat. "If you don't stop right now then. . . ." Limits are to teach our children about important life lessons like self-control and managing their feelings, not about manipulating their behavior.

Adapt your parenting strategies or expectations to eliminate unnecessary conflict. Dr. John Gottman, researcher and author, observed that parents initiate eighty-five percent of conflict between parent and teen. Usually the parent has an agenda and if the teen does not conform, conflict arises. When parents place their agenda on their teen it violates the boundary of the teen.

During the course of setting limits, when tensions run high and your teen begins to shout, don't mirror his behavior. Instead you might say, "Johnny, we are unable to continue this talk because we are not hearing each other. I can't hear you when you are yelling. Let's take a break and cool down and when you are ready to talk and not yell we can continue."

3. *Choose wisely when to apply a consequence, and when not to.* When a limit is violated, you don't always need to apply a disciplinary consequence. It may be enough to express your displeasure or disapproval and talk about the issue. When there is a relationship of love, understanding, and respect between parent and teen, the desire to keep the relationship intact will be a strong motivating factor for the adolescent. He will not want to lose your love and respect. At other times, when your kids are fighting and putting each other down, it may not be enough to say, "Stop calling each other names. In this family we respect one another." A disciplinary consequence may be necessary to lead to a change in behavior.

When Vincent was a sophomore in high school, he was going through a particularly difficult adolescent developmental period, which is a euphemism for saying that he was being a jerk! He was rude and disrespectful to his mother, and was constantly teasing his brother and sister. His parents used the broken record technique, reminding him again and again that his teasing was hurtful, and that the disrespectful behavior needed to stop. Eventually it got so bad that Vincent's parents decided to establish a limit with a clear consequence. Something had to be done to make a stronger statement. Vincent was unaware of how his negative attitude was affecting everyone, so his parents dangled the carrot of the driver's license.

Vincent was almost sixteen and couldn't wait to get his license. His parents told him that if he was not more respectful of family members then they would have to postpone him getting his license. It was important for him to be able to have more control over his aggressive behavior; otherwise he might be a danger on the road. It turned out that Vincent's parents postponed his license for two weeks. His teasing of his brother and sister didn't cease altogether, but it did lessen.

Establishing limits and avoiding the extremes of being too permissive or too strict is part of the challenge of parenting teenagers. To paraphrase the poet Robert Frost, Strong fences make strong neighbors. And healthy limit-setting makes healthy families.

Helping Your Teenager Succeed in School

Michelle came to my classroom one day after school to discuss concerns about her son. She opened with a fairly common parenting complaint, "Andrew isn't doing his homework. His grades are terrible. He's a smart boy and has scored in the ninetieth percentile on his standardized tests. He just isn't doing his work. What can I do?"

Many parents share Michelle's frustrations. What can I do to help my child be successful in school? How do I get my kid to do his homework? How should I respond to a poor report card? Some parents assume they know what the problem is—he wastes time, he's lazy, he spends too much time on the computer—and their solution is to take away rather than steer toward needed resources. They begin purging privileges. They take away the computer, the cell phone, the TV, the video games . . . everything. Unfortunately, in the majority of cases, this withdrawal of privileges does very little to motivate the unwilling student.

Rebecca's father wasn't much different. When she brought home a report card of three C's, two D's, and an F, he exploded. He took away the use of the computer, cell phone, and her ipod. He made her quit the cheerleading squad. She had to come home right after school and wasn't allowed to hang out with her friends. Soon, there was nothing left for Rebecca to lose. And predictably, her grades did not improve.

Some parents try to motivate their kids by comparing them with siblings or friends. "Why can't you get the grades your brother earned?" or, "Your cousin is a good student; what happened to you?" This approach does not work either.

All the yelling, screaming, shaming, comparing, pleading, begging, punishing, lecturing, or anger in the world will not make your child be successful in the classroom.

Research findings by the Search Institute indicate that for most kids parental support for school success is lacking. In their study of over one hundred thousand teenagers, fewer than a third said "yes" when asked: "Are your parents actively involved in helping you succeed in school?"

Parents of high school students often wonder how involved they should be in their teens' lives. What should I expect with regard to my child's grades? How do I handle a poor attitude toward learning? What if my daughter gets poor grades and is not working up to her potential? What if my son does not get involved in any clubs or extracurricular activities? What if my child isn't making any friends? Should I intervene or should I leave my teenager alone to figure things out?

> Research suggests that the more a parent is involved in his or her child's academic life, the greater the chances of that child's success in school.

There are no easy answers to these questions. Each child is unique and every situation is different. However, one basic rule holds true. Research suggests that the more a parent is involved in his or her child's academic life, the greater the chances of that child's success in school. The most influential involvement is the type that actually draws parents physically into the school, attending school programs and extra-curricular activities. When parents take the time to attend a school function, they communicate to their kids a strong message about the value of education. Teenagers pick up on this.

Three steps parents can take to help teens succeed in school:

1. *Attend school functions.* Make it a priority to attend school programs, such as Back-to-School Night, Open House, PTA meetings, and parent-teacher conferences. Support

extracurricular activities, such as speech tournaments, school plays and concerts, and sporting events.

Laurence Steinberg, a Temple University psychologist, writes: "When parents take the time to attend a school function—time off from an evening activity or time off from their own jobs—they send a strong message about how important school is to them, and by extension, how important it should be to the child." Many parents attend these programs when their kids are in elementary and middle school but stop when their kids are in high school. They presume that their children don't want them to attend once they reach high school age. Don't fall into this trap. Your participation in school programs is a great way to support your teen's success in school.

2. *Get to know your child's teachers and form a working relationship with them.* Be a partner in your teen's education by forming a working relationship with his teachers. Communicate with the teacher to stay on top of any trouble spots, either socially or academically. Use the phone or e-mail to keep in touch. Steve has parents who e-mail him and ask about the progress of their child. This helps the parents stay informed, and it also keeps him more aware of that student.

> Parents, regardless of what you know or don't know or even what you think you don't know, you are still capable of helping your child with her homework.

Mary attended Back-to-School Night and introduced herself to each of her daughter's teachers. She mentioned that she would be contacting them. A week later she followed up with an e-mail to say hello. Four weeks into the semester she e-mailed again and inquired about the progress of her daughter. This helped her stay informed, but more important, when her daughter began to slip, her English teacher contacted Mary immediately. Since the relationship had already been established, the teacher was more inclined to contact her when a problem arose.

3. *Give guidance with homework.* We have to admit that this is easier for parents of younger children. Most elementary school kids respond well to having their parents give them a spelling test, quiz them on vocabulary words, or work with them with their multiplication flash cards.

It is a myth that all high school students no longer want or need their parents' help with homework. Sure, some teenagers will refuse to accept help, even when they obviously need it. But others are able to ask for help and appreciate having their parents' involvement.

Parents, regardless of what you know or don't know or even what you think you don't know, you are still capable of helping your child with her homework. All you have to be is caring, concerned, involved, and willing to invest time with your student.

Tips for parents:

- *Review tests that are brought home for a signature.* When your daughter comes home with a test or quiz that requires a parent signature, stop before you sign your name. Review with your child the problems that she missed. In this way you are teaching her the important lesson of learning from her mistakes.

- *Proofread papers.* If you are proficient in English, correct the grammar mistakes that you find. If you are not very good at grammar and spelling, read the paper for content and give your son feedback as to the ideas that he has incorporated into his essay.

- *Quiz your teens.* When your daughter has an upcoming test, offer to quiz her on the subject matter, whether it be

Spanish vocabulary words, history questions, or English grammar rules.

- *Brainstorm ideas for projects and papers.* When your son needs a topic for his science project, a theme for a fiveparagraph essay, or a topic for his history term paper, offer to brainstorm ideas with him. Help him research materials for his project. Help him to formulate the main ideas for his term paper.

It's true that some teenagers will not want their parents to help with school work, whereas others will welcome your involvement. You cannot force your teenagers to accept your help. The important thing is to make the offer, and then let your teenager decide whether he wants to take you up on your offer, or not.

Our daughter's school requires a senior service project, and the project proposal was due in April of her junior year. Patt brainstormed with Mikhaila ideas for the project. Eventually she settled on the idea of collecting used books for the students of a local private middle school for low-income students. Mikhaila wrote a rough draft of her proposal and Patt reviewed it with her, making suggestions for revising the wording. With input and support from her mom, Mikhaila wrote an excellent proposal, and she was eager to get started on her project.

An important rule with regard to helping with homework: Work with your teen; do not do the work for them. If they get stuck, help them get unstuck, but do not take over and do the work for them.

No guarantees

Even if involved parents do all these things, there is no guarantee that their teenager is going to be successful in school. It is essential to keep in mind that your son or daughter's success in school may have little to do with your being a good or bad parent. It has much more to do with the temperament, talents, and personality of your child. Even within the same family there may be a variety of learners. One child may be a high achiever, earning mostly A's, while another child may not have much interest in school, bringing home mediocre grades.

Responding to the unmotivated student

Let's return to the opening story about the parent who is concerned about her son's grades and study habits. What can parents do to motivate the underachieving student?

Removing privileges is often counterproductive, as is trying to shame our kids into success by comparing them to others. Continually nagging or using intimidation about homework doesn't work either. It is disrespectful and mean. Nor is it advisable to simply ignore the situation.

Educators have been speculating for years why some students are self-motivated and others are not. Lack of motivation and student apathy is a serious problem in schools today. In *How to Raise a Child with a High EQ: A Parents' Guide to Emotional Intelligence*, Lawrence Shapiro offers some concrete answers about how to develop self-motivation in students. His general principals are:

- teaching your child to expect success,

- providing opportunities for your child to master his world,

- making education relevant to your child's interests and style of learning,

- teaching your child to value persistent effort, and

- teaching your child the importance of facing and overcoming failure.

Five tips for parents of a non-motivated or underachieving student:

1. *Maintain the emotional connection with your teenager.* Don't let homework battles ruin your emotional bond. Focus

Most teachers are more than willing to help the struggling student. However, it is very difficult for the average high school student to approach his teacher and ask for help.

on the bigger issue of tapping into the core reasons for low motivation. Remind yourself that a caring relationship with your son or daughter is more important than their poor grades. This may be hard for some parents, since they are so acutely aware of the importance of good grades for their child's future. If you focus only on the poor grades and not on the feelings that underlie the lack of motivation, you will get into a control battle with your teen. If the consequences that you establish—removing privileges, restricting time with friends, not allowing participation on sports teams—destroys your relationship, then you may win the battle but lose the war, and the deeper issues underlying the low motivation may never be truly addressed.

2. *Encourage your child to talk to his teacher and ask for guidance.* Most teachers are more than willing to help the struggling student. However, it is very difficult for the average high school student to approach his teacher and ask for help. If a student does take the initiative to talk to his teacher, the teacher can offer suggestions and guidance, perhaps even opportunities for extra credit work. This may provide the extra support the student needs to become motivated to improve.

When our daughter earned a "C" grade on a history test, we investigated the problem together. She recognized that she didn't do well on the essay portion of the test. We encouraged her to talk with the teacher and seek information about what she might do to improve her essay-writing skills. Mikhaila summoned up the courage to contact her history teacher. The teacher set up a time to meet with Mikhaila to give her the extra help she needed. Many students have a very difficult time requesting help, yet it is an important skill to learn. It was a significant step for Mikhaila to approach her teacher and ask.

3. *Set up a meeting with your child's teacher to assess the problem areas and work toward solutions.* Some students lack motivation when they are unable to master the material. Meet with the teacher to help assess what the problems might be: Is the material too difficult? Does the student not understand the concepts? Is it a matter of poor study skills? Is there a learning challenge? Is it a self-esteem issue? Brainstorm with the teacher strategies for improvement and focus on finding resources that will help the student experience success. Be sure to include your teenager in this meeting, and ask her what she thinks she may need to improve.

4. *Chart a course of action.* Once you have assessed the situation, take action. Is your daughter struggling because she doesn't understand the material? Then don't ground her; get a tutor. Is your son spending too much time on the computer playing games and IM-ing friends? Then design a time for homework only, setting aside a specific amount of time each evening for homework without distractions. Agree to rules like: During the homework time there is no TV, no computer, no video games. When the time is over, your son may use his computer to communicate with friends or play games. He may watch TV or just hang out.

5. *Remind your teen to stay the course.* This is a very difficult middle ground to walk. It can be helpful to remind your teen to do his homework, but you don't want to constantly nag him. One father confided: "I ask my son once in a while if his homework is done. In reality, I mention it to him about once in every five or six times

it crosses my mind. And my son still says to me, 'Dad, you're always nagging me about my homework.'"

On the other hand, if we keep reminding and nagging our kids about doing their homework, it makes homework our problem rather than theirs. Kids reason, "I don't have to worry about homework, because my parents are worrying about it for me." In these cases, challenge yourself to back off and give the burden of responsibility back to the teen. When we take responsibility for their work, it sends a message that they are incapable, and we have to do it for them.

Our middle child often needed reminders about doing his homework. During his senior year we decided it was time to put the onus on him to complete his work in a timely manner. We stopped checking up on him, stopped asking, "Do you have any homework? Did you get your homework done?" Paul responded by earning the best grades he had gotten in all four years in high school. His 3.5 GPA was a testimony to his maturity, as well as to the effectiveness of supporting him in taking responsibility for his school work.

You can lead a horse to water

It is certainly frustrating and disheartening for parents when their kids perform poorly in school. Motivating an underachieving student is one of the most challenging tasks facing parents of teens. It demands patience, flexibility, and creativity. Even when parents do all that they can, kids may still not respond. It is important for parents not to blame themselves for their child's lack of motivation and lack of achievement in school. Parents can only do so much; the rest is up to the kids.

We are reminded of that age-old proverb, "You can lead a horse to water, but you can't make him drink." This saying hits the mark when applied to motivating the underachieving student. Explore all avenues that are open to you, and then let go. Realize that your child is the one who must ultimately take responsibility for his choices, even the poor ones. Have faith that you have done your best and trust that your support and your involvement will ultimately bear fruit in unexpected ways. Who knows? Even if you can't make the horse drink, you might be able to make him thirsty.

Behind the Wheel

It happened for the second time in my life just this past January. Our teenage son had gotten his driver's permit only a few hours earlier and begged to go practice. So I ventured off, risking life and limb.

Hey, in all fairness, everything went fine—at least from the time he started the car until the time he backed it out of the driveway. But after rounding the first corner, the situation began to deteriorate.

Glancing over his left shoulder to make a lane change, Paul swerved the car into the right lane. My knuckles turned white from clutching the handle above my door, I noticed I wasn't breathing. From previous experience I know the importance of not overreacting with a student driver, so I positioned myself where I could grab the steering wheel to help him out if needed. After we were just a few blocks away I suggested that we return home. I calmly affirmed his lesson for the day. "Good job, son," I said firmly, concealing my nervousness.

Every day, high school students across the United States pass their driver's test and earn a license. It is a right of passage for teenagers. But this does not necessarily mean they are ready to drive safely and responsibly. Parents are the key in teaching their kids how to steer clear of irresponsible driving.

The first step in teaching your teenager to be a good driver is for you to model responsibility behind the wheel. Do you exercise courtesy when you drive? How about the last time you were cut off by an unaware driver, did you model tolerance? Do you routinely wear your seat belt, drive safely, and obey all traffic laws? Do you drive cautiously near schools and in neighborhoods? Are you able to de-escalate aggressive confrontations by ignoring hostile gestures or by avoiding eye contact? Do you drink and drive? These are important questions to ask and to answer honestly. More often than not, kids do as we do, not as we say. Our example teaches children, without lecturing, how to drive safely.

Our kids can also learn from our mistakes. Share with them about tickets or traffic accidents you have had in the past, and what you have learned from them.

Steering the course

Many parents dread the huge responsibility of their teenager getting the driver's license.

A parent's greatest nightmare is that their child will be killed in a car accident. Cars are more deadly than firearms in the hands of teens. The number one cause of death and injury for teenagers is car accidents. That is what we fear most and want to protect our kids from. The National Institute of Child Health and Human Development reports that high risk behaviors that lead to car accidents can be significantly reduced when parents set limits and take an active interest in teaching their adolescent how to be a safe driver.

What you can do to make your teen a safer driver:

Most new drivers have no problems steering and maneuvering a car. What beginning drivers need is plenty of supervised practice before and after the license. They need practice in being able to visually scan a scene for potential danger and in making swift judgment calls to keep them safe. The following are often overlooked opportunities to give young drivers the experience and knowledge they need to be equipped licensed drivers:

1. *Believe in your teenager and trust in his ability to be a responsible driver.*

> High risk behaviors that lead to car accidents can be significantly reduced when parents set limits and take an active interest in teaching their adolescent how to be a safe driver.

Implant the words, "You are going to be a good driver, it is just a question of learning how" in his head by saying it to him often.

2. *Discuss the real safety issues about drinking and driving.* Tell your teen clearly not to mix drugs and alcohol with driving. Combining drug use with teenagers' driving inexperience and risk-taking behavior is a recipe for disaster. Some teens have the belief that smoking marijuana does not impair driving ability. This is not true, so include marijuana use in your talks. For more information read the chapter titled "Teens and Marijuana."

3. *Have a game plan.* Does your daughter know what to do if she has been drinking and knows that it is unsafe to drive? Consider making a written pledge that you will pick her up anytime, anywhere—no questions asked—if she calls for a ride home because of alcohol and/or drug use. You want her to be physically safe.

4. *Practice the unexpected.* The first ticket one of our three adolescent drivers received was for using a left-turn center lane. He was supposed to turn left, yet he drove straight ahead. It was very confusing for our novice driver. He had never come across a situation like that and was thrown off. Here is a list of other situations that can easily be overlooked. Consider practicing:

- on one-way streets
- in rush hour
- in city traffic
- in inclement weather
- nighttime driving
- merging lanes
- on country roads
- on gravel roads

- with a stick shift
- on poor road conditions
- while changing lanes
- in mountains/hills

5. *Discuss car rules ahead of time.* This includes what are the basic speed limits on all types of streets and highways. Don't assume your son or daughter already knows them. Voice your expectations before the permit is earned, and spell out the guidelines when the license comes.

Parents will be faced with a flood of new issues that require decisions on their part. In the accompanying chart are some things to think about. Decide as a couple how you want to handle them with your teen driver. When you are clear, begin discussing them with your teen. Otherwise, you may be caught off guard when you are faced with them.

Supervision	Remind your driver that you will still need to know where he is going, with whom, what kinds of activities have been planned, and what time he will return home.
Availability	Spell out when the car will be available for use. Your teen must let you know in advance before taking the car.
Driving hours	Identify what hours driving is permitted and not permitted.
Curfew	Many states limit what time your teen can drive at night, but if yours does not, consider the recommendation of AAA. They suggest a curfew of 10 p.m. or 11 p.m. for teen drivers.
Passengers	The more kids in a car, the greater the chance of an accident. Some states have a blacked-out period where newly licensed teen drivers are restricted from transporting passengers. Talk about when you will allow others in the car and under what circumstances. Permit your son or daughter to take no more passengers than the car has functioning seat belts.

Drinking and driving	Young drivers expect and want their parents to talk to them about the issue of drinking and driving. Let them know how you feel and what your concerns are. Clearly state what you expect from them. (As we stated above, consider making a written agreement that you will pick up your teen anytime, anywhere, no questions asked, if they call for a ride home because of alcohol and/or drug use.)
Steering clear of pot	Research indicates that one in six high school students report driving under the influence of marijuana. Accident rates for teens under the influence of marijuana are the same as for those who drink and drive. Handle this the same way as drinking.
When plans change	Plan ahead for unforeseen problems. Remind your teens to call when their plans change or if they need your help.
Cell phone usage	Talking on the phone while driving is dangerous. Suggest that cell phone usage be prohibited unless it is an emergency. Have it be for communication only, not conversation.
General car usage	Make it clear who pays for gas and who is responsible for keeping the car clean.
Letting friends drive	Let your teens know that the car is not to be lent to anyone without your permission.
Incentives and tickets	Reward your teen if the first twelve months of driving are ticket- and accident-free. The flip side is that if there is a ticket within the first six months, then driving privileges will be forfeited for a period of time. You may want to spell this one out in writing so everyone is clear on the agreement.
Grades and insurance	Rates can double or triple when adding a teen driver. Often there are premium discounts for students with good grades. Ask your agent how your teen may qualify and communicate the stipulations to your son or daughter.
Celebrate success	Acknowledge and reward good driving and drug-free behavior.

6. *In case of accidents.* Have you discussed with your young driver what to do in case of an accident? In crisis

situations we can be nervous and not think clearly. In our family, we put in the glove compartment of every car a form called "What to Do in Case of an Accident. It is to be filled out in case of an accident." We put the form and a pen in an envelope. This makes things easy. They just need to gather the information by filling in the blanks. It includes things like:

1. Remain calm and move your car to a safe and visible place.

2. Even if you are responsible for the accident, do not admit this to another driver or police until you have contacted your insurance agent. Do not sign anything unless it is for the police or your insurance company.

3. Call police immediately, even if the accident seems minor.

4. Record the other car's make, model, and license plate number.

5. Get the driver's name, address, phone number including area code, license number, name of insurance company, and insurance company policy number.

6. If the driver is not the owner of the car, get the owner's name/address/phone number.

7. Record the names and addresses of other passengers or witnesses.

8. Record specific details: accident circumstances, time of day, location, weather conditions, visibility, and any other important information.

9. Keep a disposable camera in the glove box and take pictures of the damage to your car and of the accident scene.

10. Notify your insurance company immediately.

Driving is a privilege, not a right. Grant privileges slowly. Allowing your teen to get her license provides the opportunity for her to demonstrate responsibility. Remind your teen that the opportunity to drive may be restricted if she is not fulfilling her responsibilities at home and school.

Our son Paul is now a full-fledged driver. We provided him with sufficient opportunity to practice good driving habits. It is remarkable how much responsibility he has demonstrated since getting his license. He is setting his alarm and getting himself up in the morning, willingly driving his sister to swim practice at 7 a.m., and using good judgment in his driving.

Parents, accept the inevitable. There will be unexpected curves ahead, but with some straight talk and planning, you can help your teen learn to be a responsible young adult driver. So hang on and enjoy the ride.

Sex Education Begins at Home

March is "Talk to Teens About Sex" month. We didn't make this up. This is a national campaign to help parents initiate discussions with their kids about sex and sexuality. My parents didn't have this kind of discussion with me, but times are very different now.

In the early '70's there were five common sexually transmitted diseases (STDs), and AIDS was unheard of. Today, there are more than twenty-five STDs, and five of them remain incurable.

In the United States alone, nearly one million people are currently living with the human immunodeficiency virus (HIV). The frightening news is that about a quarter of them do not even know that they are infected. In the year 2002 an estimated fifty thousand new cases of AIDS were diagnosed among adults and adolescents. HIV/AIDS is only one of the many physical and emotional risks associated with sexual involvement. Sexual activity comes with a price tag, and we need to inform our youth of the costs.

Now you know why having a "Talk to Teens About Sex" month is so important. We have to educate our kids about the dangerous emotional, physical, and spiritual consequences of engaging in premarital sex. The coaching needs to be ongoing and not just during the month of March. Have you been dialoguing with your kids?

In a recent survey of high school seniors only a third said that their parents talked to them about sexual issues. The statistics were only slightly better when freshmen were surveyed. Less than half reported they had discussed sex with their parents. In a study by the California Wellness Foundation, 65

Sexual activity comes with a price tag, and we need to inform our youth of the costs.

percent of the adults reported that they had talked with their children about sex, but only 41 percent of the kids seem to have heard that discussion. The problem is that the message delivered is not always the message received.

If kids are not hearing about sex from parents, then where are they getting their information? You guessed it, first from the media. Then from their peers, who, of course, get their information from the media. Every day the media bombards us with messages that sex is casual, everybody's doing it, and there are no consequences. In one year of prime-time television, there are approximately 20,000 individual scenes of suggested sexual behavior, most of which is between non-married couples. These programs rarely portray the very real dangers of casual sexual intimacy.

Why is it so difficult to have conversations with our kids about sex?

One reason why we fail to talk to our kids about sex is because we have no model. For many of us our parents didn't even broach the subject. A second reason is embarrassment. Plain and simple, we are self-conscious and so are our teens. It is uncomfortable to talk about sex. Third, fear. Some believe by discussing human sexuality or by giving accurate information it will encourage kids to engage in sex. Nothing could be further from the truth. Teens who have accurate information and understand what is really at stake are more likely to wait to have sex.

Research is finding that adolescents who discuss topics of sexuality with parents are more likely to delay sex, and among sexually active youths, they are more likely to protect themselves by using contraception.

How much influence do parents really have? More than you know. A national survey by the National Campaign to Prevent Teen Pregnancy (NCPTP) found that a parent's influence is even stronger than peers'. Teens reported that they were definitely influenced by their friends' opinions when they decided to have sex, but when asked which forces were most influential in preventing premature sexual activity, teens rated parents first. When parents were asked the same question, they assumed they had less influence. Half of the parents believed friends had the greater influence.

Parents, your thoughts and opinions matter. You have significant influence on your teens' attitudes and choices about whether or not they become sexually active. A 2003 study from the University of Minnesota found that the more a child believes that Mom and Dad disapprove of them having sex, the less likely they are to do it.

Five steps to influence your teen's sexual decision-making:

1. *Talk, talk, then talk some more.* Having a one-time "sex talk" is not enough for the teens of today. Hold ongoing conversations about issues of sexuality and sexual expression and relationship. Start early and be age appropriate. Ask them questions that provoke thought. Make comments that tweak their interest and get them to think. Ask and then listen. We want teens to think about what possible consequences their actions today may have on their future.

By "conversations" we mean an exchange of thoughts, feelings, and stories. Share on a real level, on an emotional level; don't just spit out facts and figures. Scaring kids will not work. Talking openly will. Processing provides them with an interpersonal experience that facilitates self-understanding.

Look for opportunities to discuss issues of sexual expression and sexual decision-making and to educate your child about healthy relationships. Here are some possibilities:

- **The daily newspapers and magazines.** Often there are articles about relationship issues. A recent *Oprah* magazine had an article about oral sex. The author mentioned that kids as young as twelve and thirteen years old were engaging in oral sex. Many teens do not consider oral sex to be "real" sex. This article would be an excellent opportunity to engage your teens in a discussion about appropriate sexual expression. Tell them your reaction to the article and ask them what they think.

- **The media.** When watching a movie or television program that has sexual content, make an observation, and then ask your kids their opinions. Listen to what they say. Some parents make the mistake of trying to stuff their agenda down their kid's throat.

  The average sitcom has twenty sexual situations or sexual innuendoes per half hour program. You can make it a game to try and count how many you recognize. You might say, "It seems to me that this program portrays sex as something totally casual. I have yet to see any real possible consequences, like pregnancy, STDs, HIV, or emotional pain. What do you notice?" *Caution*: When asking questions wait until commercial. I have been banned from the family room because my teens say I interrupt too much.

- **Drawing from the experiences of others.** A relative has an abortion, a teenage cousin fathers a child, a neighborhood girl acts out sexually— these are opportunities to discuss with your teens their feelings and views and to share your own. Mrs. Smith commented on the behavior of one of her daughter's friends: "I'm concerned about Marla and her self-respect. Having sex with her boyfriend after knowing him for two weeks doesn't reflect good judgment. What do you think?"

- **One-on-one time with your teenager.** Initiate a conversation while driving. Sometimes good discussions happen while driving because little or no eye contact has to be made. Going out to lunch, playing sports together, or going on a camping trip together are other advantageous times to dialogue about important issues. Don't talk at your teen. Talk with each other and make it personal.

> Teach them what is really at stake. Empower your kids so that they can make an informed decision about their sexual behavior.

2. *Be clear about your values.* Be unambiguous about communicating what is important to you. Society and youth culture give confusing messages about the casualness of sex, and parents need to clearly state the sacredness of sex and the place of sexual intercourse within the commitment of marriage.

Research is supporting the importance of parents sharing their values. A 2000 study done by the National Teen Pregnancy Prevention Research Center analyzed interviews of over three thousand students in grades eight to eleven and their mothers. One group of teens had moms who disapproved of them having sex, while another group had moms who did not express disapproval. Follow-up interviews a year later showed that girls whose mothers shared their values and educated their daughters were more likely to remain sexually inactive.

3. *Educate yourselves about the very real dangers of adolescents having premature sexual intercourse.* Then educate your teens. Teach them what is really at stake. Empower your kids so that they can make an informed decision about their sexual behavior. Some important topics for review include:

- **Teen pregnancies.** The United States continues to have the highest teen pregnancy rate in the industrialized world. According to a 2002 article in

U.S. News and World Report, one in five sexually active teenage girls gets pregnant each year.

- **Sexually transmitted diseases.** STDs are an epidemic in this country. According to a 1998 study by the Kaiser Family Foundation, more than 65 million Americans are infected with an incurable sexually transmitted disease. Adolescents are becoming infected faster than any age group with over three million new infections each year. The most widespread STD is chlamydia, which can cause pelvic inflammatory disease in females that can lead to scarring of the fallopian tubes and ultimately infertility. These are just a few of the many facts that informed and educated parents can communicate to their children.

- **Physical and emotional harm.** One of the causes of today's higher suicide rate among teens is the emotional devastation that can come from teenagers having a sexual relationship and then breaking up. The average teen couple breaks up only three weeks after having sexual intercourse for the first time.

- **Substitution of intercourse for intimacy.** We all want to be loved and cared for by others. There are many different types of intimacy in a relationship, not just sexual. One very important type of intimacy involves a deep emotional sharing with another person, and it is vital to a healthy marriage. When teenagers engage in premarital sexual activity, they often focus on the sex to the detriment of the relationship. They may stop sharing their deeper selves, and instead make the sexual connection the goal of the relationship. The sex becomes a substitute for intimacy and the relationship suffers.

4. *Put systems in place to help keep your kids safe.* Set limits and establish family rules that will support your kids in not having sex as teenagers. Some suggestions:

- **Share time together as a family.** Foster strong bonds with your kids. Share a family meal together as often as possible. Adding to the findings from "The Dinner Table" chapter (page 55): Teenagers from homes where the family eats meals together two times a week are four times less likely to have premarital sex than teens who never share a family meal.

- **Establish an age when your children can begin dating.** Ingrain early in your children that dating is a right of passage. It is best to decide before the teen years the age at which your children can begin dating. Individual dating varies depending on the circumstances and the maturity of the child. Keep in mind that there is a huge maturity difference between freshmen and seniors. Some parents set the age for one-on-one dating at age sixteen, while others establish an older age. Some parents have the rule that the person their child is dating cannot be more than two years older. You need to decide what is right for your family.

  Research indicates that a serious boyfriend or girlfriend relationship for teens under the age of sixteen increases the likelihood that they will engage in sex.

- **Minimize the time that your teenagers are home alone.** If you cannot be with them after school because of work schedules, try to arrange for another adult to be present until you get home. Teens still need supervision. Many parents have a rule that there can be no friends at the house while the parents are not home. On the flip side, friends are always welcome when the parents *are* at home.

- **Take serious action for lying.** Sometimes teenagers tell us that they are going to a friend's house, but they go somewhere else instead, for example, to an unchaperoned party. When you catch your teenager in a lie, treat it very seriously. Suspend driving privileges, for example.

5. *Be an anchor.* Let your kids know that if they make a regrettable decision, you will still love and support them, and help them deal with the consequences of their poor choice. Tell them if they choose to go against the expectations you hold for them, and they get "in trouble" that you will be there to support them, love them, and do what you can to help them through the experience. Assure your teen that you will get through this together.

Some parents believe that it does not matter what they say, and that teenagers will do whatever they want anyway. It is true that teens will make their own decisions, but it is also true that we parents have a profound influence on them.

Kids need guidance and want direction from parents. If we communicate from the heart, share our values and expectations, set appropriate limits, and continue to dialogue about issues of sexual expression, they are more likely to choose not to have premarital sex. If we give them no guidance, they will have to discover things on their own.

Parenting a teenager takes a tremendous amount of courage. And it takes more than courage to raise a healthy child. It requires us to be there in ways we never imagined.

Get talking. It's later than you think.

Teens and Marijuana

Bob had given his seventeen-year-old son, Jason, his credit card to buy gas. Jason forgot to return it. The next day while his son was at basketball practice, Bob realized that Jason still had his card. He opened Jason's backpack looking for it. He didn't find the credit card, but what he did find shocked him. Bob discovered a small plastic container stuffed with marijuana. He had no hint that his son was smoking marijuana. When Bob confronted his son, Jason was defensive and unrepentant. He told his dad that all his friends smoked marijuana, and that it was actually safer than drinking.

"Everyone smokes marijuana, Dad. It's no big deal."

That is not what the experts are saying. Research summarized by the National Youth Anti-Drug Media Campaign underscores the frightening trends in marijuana perception and use by today's teens. (See www.TheAntiDrug.com.)

Marijuana is the most commonly used illegal drug in this country. Since the 1990s, marijuana use has almost doubled among younger teens. Accompanying this upward pattern is significant erosion in anti-drug perceptions and knowledge among teenagers. As the number of young people who use marijuana has increased, those who view the drug as harmful has decreased.

Contrary to popular belief, the majority of teenagers do not use marijuana. Among students surveyed in an annual national survey, only about one in five sophomores reported they are current marijuana users. That is defined by using marijuana within the past month. Fewer than one in four high school seniors report that they are current marijuana users. But, the number of students who have tried marijuana is up significantly. Forty percent of preteens and teens reported that they have experimented with marijuana, and half of all graduating seniors.

Marijuana can be addictive

Long-term marijuana use can lead to addiction in some people. Addiction is defined as the inability to control the urges to seek out and use marijuana, even though it negatively affects family relationships, school performance, and recreational activities. According to one study, marijuana use by teenagers who have prior antisocial problems can quickly lead to addiction. In addition, some frequent, heavy marijuana users develop "tolerance" to its effects. This means they need larger and larger amounts of marijuana to get the same desired effects as they used to get from smaller amounts.

More teens enter treatment for marijuana dependence than for all other illicit drugs combined. The more a teen uses the drug the greater the chances that he or she will develop dependency. Adolescents who smoke marijuana are more at risk for dependency than adults.

Marijuana is harmful. Longitudinal research on marijuana users has shown that they have lower achievement in many areas than non-users, more acceptance of deviant behavior, more delinquent behavior and aggression, greater rebelliousness, poorer relationships with parents, and more associations with delinquent and drug-using friends. In addition, smoking marijuana decreases energy and ambition and shortens attention span. For young users, marijuana can lead to increased anxiety, panic attacks, depression, and other health problems.

According to The National Household Survey on Drug Abuse, adolescents who smoke marijuana are nine times more likely than non-users to experiment with other illegal drugs or alcohol, five times more likely to steal, and nearly four times more likely to be violent.

Why do kids smoke marijuana?

Youth start using marijuana for many reasons. All aspects of a child's environment—home, school, and neighborhood—may influence their choice to experiment with drugs. Curiosity and the desire to fit in with a social group are common reasons. Thinking it is enjoyable is another. Some turn to drugs to self-medicate deep psychological pain. Some kids use marijuana as a way to cope with their anxiety, anger, or depression. The use of alcohol and drugs by other family members plays a strong role in whether children start using drugs.

Parents have the greatest influence on a child's decision to get involved with drugs. There is a growing body of evidence that shows that parents are central to preventing adolescent substance abuse. Statistics show that kids whose parents talk to them regularly about the dangers of drugs are almost fifty percent less likely to use drugs. In fact, kids themselves say that losing their parents' trust and respect are the most important reasons not to use drugs. As a parent, your actions do matter.

When you suspect, or know, that your child has used drugs, take action to stop it immediately. It may be one of the most important steps you ever take. The following are some clues of possible drug use that parents can watch for in their teenagers. By observing you can learn a lot. You want to recognize trouble before it goes too far.

Seven warning signs that may indicate drug involvement:

1. *Decline in school performance.* A drop in grades, incomplete work, excuses for poor performance, absenteeism or truancy, cutting classes, resentment toward teachers or authority figures, sleeping

> Kids themselves say that losing their parents' trust and respect are the most important reasons not to use drugs.

or daydreaming in class, or being non-responsive in class are often signs of drug use.

2. *Change in personal appearance.* Look for a change in clothing style, drug-related clothing and jewelry, poor personal hygiene, sloppy appearance, tattoos, change in weight, an unsteady gait, smell of alcohol or pot, slurred speech, giddiness, bloodshot eyes, or dilated pupils.

3. *Variations in behavior.* When a person is using drugs, you may notice that he or she is angry or hostile, short-tempered, verbally or physically abusive, apathetic, generally more unhappy, easily upset, unmotivated, less energetic, or sleeping more. In addition, the person may display emotional highs and lows not typical for that person, poor nutritional habits, and may smell of alcohol or marijuana.

4. *More secretive and private.* Signs to watch for: aloofness, withdrawl from responsibilities and family, less contact with old friends, more time spent alone.

5. *Change in peers.* Replaces lifelong friends with new friends you don't know, no longer introduces friends, receives mysterious phone calls, associates with friends who are known drug users, is suddenly popular with older kids, talks of drugs or parties.

6. *Unusual patterns of behavior.* Vague physical symptoms and complaints, headaches, stomach cramps, nauseous, up late, irregular and excessive sleeping habits, secretive phone calls, preoccupation with death and suicide, reduced memory or attention span, overtired or excessive energy, sudden drop in grades, selling of possessions, uses eye drops or room deodorizers, unexplained money or merchandise from unknown sources, drug paraphernalia such as rolling papers, pipes, or roach clips.

7. *Defensive and guarded attitude about drugs.* Tells you everybody is doing it and that it is "natural." Or asks, "Didn't you use drugs when you were my age?"

If you suspect drug use, talk directly to your teen about your observations and concerns. You may want to involve a health professional and take your child to his or her doctor. Ask about an evaluation for drugs and alcohol. Some of these signs also indicate there may be a deeper problem with depression, gang involvement, or suicidal thoughts, and professional screening may be helpful.

Five things that parents can do when their child is using:

1. *Get educated.* First, learn as much as you can. Today's marijuana is much more potent than the marijuana of the past. Educate yourself about the harmful effects of the drug, and what you can do to steer your kids away from marijuana use. Turn to local resources or sign up for The-AntiDrug.com biweekly e-mail newsletter. They share in-depth information and the latest research on drug and alcohol use by teens. They give suggestions for action steps parents can take. You can call the National Clearinghouse for Alcohol and Drug Information (NCADI) for free pamphlets and fact sheets. Another excellent resource is the Partnership for a Drug-Free America.

2. *Talk to your teen. Let him know you know.* Be sure to have the conversation when you are calm and have plenty of time. This isn't an easy task; your feelings may range from anger to sadness to guilt that you have "failed" because your kid is using drugs. This isn't true. By staying involved you can help him stop using and make choices that will make a positive difference in his life. Be specific about your concerns. Tell your child what you see and how you feel about it. Be specific about the things you have observed that cause concern. Make it known if you found evidence, such as drug paraphernalia, empty bottles, or disguised liquor. Identify for him exactly how his

behavior or appearance has changed and why that worries you. Tell him that drug and alcohol use is dangerous for his development, and it's your job to keep him away from things that put him in danger.

Have this discussion without getting mad or accusing your child of being stupid or bad or an embarrassment to the family. Be firm but loving with your tone, and do not get hooked into an argument. He will put up a fight, but you do not need to argue. Knowing that kids are naturally private about their lives, attempt to reach out. Find out what is going on in your child's life. Try not to make the discussion an inquisition; simply try to connect with your teen and identify the deeper core issues that are influencing his poor choices. Find out if friends or others offered your child drugs at a party or school. Did he try it just out of curiosity, or did he use marijuana or alcohol for some other reason? That alone will be a signal to your child that you care and that you are going to be the parent.

Be prepared for your teen to deny using drugs. Do not expect her to admit she has a problem. Your child will probably get angry and even try to change the subject. Maybe you will be confronted with questions about what you did as a teen. If you are asked, be honest and connect your use to negative consequences. Answering deceptively will cause you to lose credibility with your kid. On the other hand, if you don't feel comfortable answering the question, you can talk about some specific people you know who have had negative things happen to them as a result of drug and alcohol use.

3. *Know where your kids are and what they're doing.* Set clear rules for your kids about what they may do and with whom they may spend time, and talk to them about why these rules are important. Establish curfews and make unchaperoned parties off-limits. Make a special effort to

know where your children and teens are on the weekends and after school, since those are the "danger zones." Unsupervised young people have more opportunities to use drugs, commit crimes, and engage in other risky behavior. Be an attentive par

> Give your teen opportunities to rebuild a trusting relationship when trust has been broken.

ent without being authoritarian, and keep track of their whereabouts. Remember, knowing where your kids are and what they're up to doesn't make you a nag; it says that you care.

4. *Take appropriate action.* Tell him that drug use will not be allowed in your home. Observe and identify what the deeper core issues are that may be influencing his poor choices. Open up healthy dialogues with your teen exploring his drug use. Try to understand the motivations behind his behavior so that you can help solve the problem. When you get a better understanding of the situation, then you can decide on the next steps. These could include setting new rules and consequences that are reasonable and enforceable—such as a new curfew, no cell phone or computer privileges for a period of time, or less time hanging out with friends. You may consider having your child see a counselor. In some cases it may be appropriate for parents to test their teenager for drugs.

5. *Share activities.* Spend time with your kids, engaged in activities that suit their ages and interests. In fact, don't work at your relationship, but play at it. Shared experiences build a bank account of affection and trust that forms the basis for future communication. Eat together because meals are a great opportunity to talk about the day's events. Use the time for conversation, not confrontation. Read, watch TV or movies, exercise, or play sports

as a family. Get involved in community service with your kids. Find ways to play together.

What's most important to bear in mind when dealing with the issue of drug use by your adolescent is the primacy of the parent-teen relationship. Give your teen opportunities to rebuild a trusting relationship when trust has been broken. Tough love may be necessary in extreme cases to keep healthy boundaries and guide your teen into making better choices for himself. Realize that the most important ally you have is a strong bond with your teen. This, more than anything, will help both parent and teen navigate this very challenging situation.

A couple decided to take their teenage daughter to a shopping mall in a nearby town one weekend.

As they were getting ready to go, the teenager came downstairs dressed in short shorts and a spaghetti string top.

An anticipated fight broke out between the girl and her father over her "inappropriate" attire.

In order to keep the peace, the mother stepped in and reminded her husband that when they were young she had dressed the same way, it was the style.

He said, "Yeah! Well if you remember right I had something to say about that, too!"

"Yes dear," she said, "You did . . . you asked me for my phone number!"

—*E-mail humor, author unknown*

PART THREE: CARING

The eyes of love see more, not less.
And because love sees more,
it is willing to notice less.

As our kids have helped us realize, even parenting experts have trouble with their teenagers.

Steve and I are outnumbered in our family. We have three teens in our home. Around Christmastime we had one of those very bad parenting weekends. Our oldest teenager would not stop bullying his younger brother, even after being told over and over to stop. Another one complained about me being a bad mom because I would not get him a cell phone like "every other kid has." And when we went to decorate our Christmas tree only one of the three teenagers wanted to participate in this ritual we have been doing since . . . forever!

"I would rather go out with my friends than be stuck at home with you!"

I felt like a total failure as a parent.

I am fully aware that my kids don't hold the patent on this type of behavior. It is a familiar parenting story. But even knowing this did not help my spirit. I was frustrated, angry, and hurt.

The holiday season is a time for giving gifts, but what I wanted to give was a boot in someone's bottom! Getting into the spirit of giving is hard when your teenagers are mean and uncooperative, and momma wants to get revenge. However, in dark moments like these we can learn lessons about caring and celebrating the light.

During the holiday season, believers of many faiths light candles to remind them of the power of light to overcome the darkness. In the same way, the power of love and caring can guide us to overcome the darkness of our kids' undesirable behaviors, or our own pissy attitudes. Love opens us to witness the light that is within. Giving the gift of caring enables us to look past our teenager's selfish behaviors in order to see the person within, whom we love. Love also allows us to forgive ourselves for our failures and imperfections. In truth, we all want to be loved and accepted. We are beings of light, valuable and worthy of love.

To maintain your sanity while parenting your teenagers, intentionally strengthen the bond with your parenting partner. The greatest gift parents can give their children is to love each other. A deep and caring parental bond is the solid foundation upon which a loving and healthy family is built.

Caring for one another—the focus of Part 3—surveys the building of wholesome and loving relationships between husbands and wives, parenting partners, mothers and daughters, fathers and sons, teenagers and parents. Included are essays on appreciating our kids, nurturing mutual respect, and teaching important life skills, such as goal-setting, effective listening, and emotional intelligence.

So when your teenagers are doing their "adolescent thing" of being demanding and uncooperative, or when a perfectly good evening has been ruined, or when you feel like a failure as a parent—pause and take a deep breath. Look at your teenager with the eyes that see more, not less, and celebrate the light that is within.

What Our Daughters Need:
Lessons on Being a Woman

As our daughter was approaching her tenth birthday I became intensely concerned with how to teach her about her femininity and what it means to be fully a woman in body, mind, heart, and soul. It is difficult growing up female in our culture. Despite all the progressive exterior changes, there is still a deep-seated belief that females are second-class citizens.

Women and men around the globe seem to have lost or forgotten the profound importance of the feminine. Sometimes I wonder what would happen if all the women of the world woke up to their own sacredness as women. We could actually transform the world.

The future of the world is in the hands of women. Women bleed the blood of life. When we bleed, it is to give birth to new life. When men bleed, they die. Sadly, what I have learned is that many people do not really even know or fully understand the depths of what it means to be a woman. This chapter shares some of that meaning. The next chapter discusses some of the qualities of fatherhood from the male (Steve's) point of view.

Being a woman conjures up negative images for many people. I had a forty-seven-year-old woman sitting in my office unable to even say out loud, "I am a woman." "I'm a girl, I'm a girl," she kept saying. "A woman is old and decrepit."

"But a girl is a child and power-less," I responded. "How will you be able to appreciate who you are if you are unable to claim it?"

> Women bleed the blood of life. When we bleed, it is to give birth to new life. When men bleed, they die.

143

Without thinking, many women refer to themselves as girls. It is cute, sweet, and nice. Like "sugar and spice." And it inadvertently keeps us vulnerable and inappropriately dependent. Girls are children, and children have little or no influence in society. Their needs are not respected and they are not even very well protected in our world. Violence against women and children has not declined in these times. If you keep referring to yourself as a girl, you are unconsciously telling yourself over and over that you are without authority and are refusing to take responsibility. You rarely hear a man refer to himself as a boy.

I know I'm asking a lot, but I want something different for my daughter and all the other daughters. What I am teaching her about herself, her body, mind, heart, and soul is daily challenged by the mainstream. Sometimes it feels like I am a salmon trying to swim upstream, back to my birth place. My mission is to guide my daughter with a depth that is not common in daily life.

The night before her tenth birthday I was startled awake in the middle of the night. It was actually 2 a.m. I suddenly shot up into a sitting position, and without thought grabbed my journal. I keep it on my nightstand, as it is not uncommon for me to have thoughts occur that are not available to me during the day. What flowed out of me that night are the following words. I have read this journal entry to wise women and they instructed me to share it.

Journal entry from the night before my daughter's tenth birthday:

> Questions and images of what it means to be a woman, to be fully feminine, engulf my thoughts and psyche. I ask myself, if I am to teach my daughter about being a woman, then I need to know what it means to be one. What have I learned about being a woman and what do I want to pass on to my daughter? More

than anything, I want her to know that real women are not afraid to celebrate the magic of being a woman.

Through prayer and meditation, I decide to turn and ask the ancestral mothers for the collective wisdom from all females who have walked before me.

I hear . . . before anything else, daughters need you to examine your own past and the lessons you have learned about what it means to be a woman. To own your deeper truth, you must speak a coherent account of your own life story so that you will not pass on to your daughter your learned fears. She needs for you to be clear, to lead, to trust what you know, to trust what you see, and to speak your truth without shrinking. Because when you get small, it not only dismisses who you are, it diminishes her power as well.

So I listen fully with my whole body, mind, heart, and soul. I listen until I receive their wisdom.

Then I speak. My daughter's femininity deserves to be remembered.

She needs me to celebrate her by listening, accepting, embracing, and seeing her for who she is, not for what I want her to be.

My daughter needs me to hold her in her pain and disappointments, and to nurture her with my comforting words and gentle touch.

I will not forget that she wants and needs for me to honor my own beauty, to embrace my femininity, and to continue to unearth it, and shed light on it. From this she will learn to honor her own beauty.

More than anything else, she needs for me to teach her the sacredness of a woman's body. For all of life depends on us. She needs for me to value and not be afraid of my sexuality. She needs for me to share with her about what I learned from my mother and what I did not learn, but needed from my mother.

I owe it to my daughter to listen to what I know and trust my intuition. Otherwise, how could I possibly teach her something I don't acknowledge?

She needs to know that I will protect her like a mama bear, and that I am able to handle chaos, transforming it into new life for her understanding.

I owe it to my daughter to model being a woman, fully human, fully sexual, passionate, creative, and expressive.

As her mother, I am able to impart profound blessings on her and I must.

She needs for me to be able to let her go and release her to other women and mothers. Most importantly she needs to know I will not abandon her under any circumstance. A mother's greatest disgrace is abandoning her daughter. The wounds go too deep to comprehend. Daughters need their mothers to teach them to be women.

Thank you mothers of the past for these ancient insights, wisdom, and knowledge. Thank you for my precious daughter and for all the ways she challenges my perceptions of what it means to be a woman. I promise to honor her femininity and promise to raise her to be a woman.

And I ask for continued courage, insight, and wisdom to be there for her in all the different ways she may need on her journey to reclaim her roots. So be it.

The Fathering Journey

When my son Brian was in fifth grade he made a Father's Day gift for me. It was his school picture along with an acrostic poem he had written, spelling out what it means to be a father. It read:

Fathers are the greatest. They
Are heroes and great to be around.
They also play with you, help you with your
Homework, and talk to you.
Everyday me and my dad do something
together. My dad is
Rad and looks young.
Sometimes people think he is 40 when his
real age is 48.

I was a hero and a great father in his eyes. But that was when he was ten years old. Then came adolescence.

As a junior in high school, Brian very much wanted a cell phone for Christmas. It was not in our thought process, budget, or plans at the time. When Santa didn't bring him one, he was furious. He threw a fit and tried hard to ruin everyone's Christmas day.

In fact, he was so angry that he ignored me and wouldn't talk to me for what seemed like weeks. When Brian was sixteen, I felt like the worst father in the universe.

They eventually do grow up

Brian is now a sophomore in college. He has grown up a lot during the past two years. When he comes home for school vacations, he is mostly enjoyable to have around. He even talks to his mother and me regularly, which was unheard of when he was in high school.

When Brian was home for spring break, he pointed out some self-centered behavior on the part of his younger brother. His brother is a junior in high school. He commented, "Paul doesn't appreciate anything you guys do for him. He's so selfish. I was never like that."

Brian had forgotten a few details from his own junior year. We hadn't.

In the meantime, I am a pretty good dad again, and feeling better about my fatherhood. The title of "World's Worst Dad" has been passed on to some other frustrated father, journeying through his parenting initiation.

Through my experiences with raising three teenagers, I have definitely been humbled and have learned many lessons.

Six lessons for being a better father

1. *Don't be so hurried.* Spend time with your teenagers. Spending time with his kids is probably the most important habit of an effective father. Many fathers let work or career interfere with this. When the kids have grown up and have left the house many dads experience the "empty nest syndrome," feeling bad about not spending more time with them while they were home. At the end of their lives, on their deathbed, very few men ever wish they had spent more time at the office.

   Take advantage of the time you have right now. Paul Lewis, author of *The Five Key Habits of Smart Dads*, writes, "What often energizes me to choose my kids instead of work is the fact that I get only one shot at my kids. They will be two years old, six years old, and ten and fourteen only once in my lifetime. If I am not there to enjoy the moment, I miss forever the opportunity of shaping a memory."

2. *Keep your eyes open.* Accept your teenager for who he is. Many kids feel that their fathers put too much pressure on them to be a certain way, to achieve straight A's, to play a particular sport. A student of mine was sharing

149

about his dad who wanted him to play baseball. The boy had played on the team throughout his four years of high school, and now it was his senior year and he confided that he *hated* playing baseball. "The only reason I do it is to make my dad happy. My dad is trying to live his dreams through me."

3. *Define your philosophy.* Paul Lewis poses this question to dads: "Do you see fathering as the work of an architect or the work of a gardener?" The architect father believes that his job is to shape his child into the individual the father wants him to be when he grows up. The man who envisions his fathering role as a gardener waters, nourishes, and tends his children as they grow. He studies them to see what is growing there, what gifts and talents they possess.

Lewis writes, "A gardener father accepts his kids for the individuals they are, celebrating the growth he sees. He is as enthusiastic about a son talented in writing as he is about the daughter on her way to an athletic scholarship, even if he was shaped in his youth by neither writing nor athletics. We all know how difficult it is not to channel our kids into the same hobbies and jobs and GPAs that worked for us in our formative years."

It is perhaps no accident that my own father, who is a magnificent gardener and previous owner of the Saso Herb Gardens in Saratoga, California, did a wonderful job of providing me with the freedom to seek my own path in life. He did not place on me expectations of what I should become or what career I should choose. He always told me, "Do what you feel called to do."

> The man who envisions his fathering role as a gardener waters, nourishes, and tends his children as they grow.

4. *Believe in your child's capabilities.* We fathers ought to have high expectations for our kids. Many of

my students tell me that they appreciate the fact that their dads have expectations for them in academics and in life. They like the fact that their dads exposed them to various sports when they were younger, and got them involved in other activities.

The fathering skill here is to recognize the difference between high expectations and unrealistic expectations. We need to strive to love our children unconditionally, to value them for who they are rather than for what they do. Instead of loving our kids based on any particular quality or competency that we wish they had, we strive to love them as they are.

5. *Listen with your eyes.* A high school senior wrote: "The most important quality of an effective father is his ability to listen to my side of the story. He doesn't jump to conclusions. He asks me first."

Mark, a freshman in high school, related that he was talking to his dad about a problem on his baseball team. The dad was watching TV. Every once in a while he would say, "Uh huh." When the son was finished, he asked his dad, "What do you think I should do?"

The dad replied, "About what?"

"Nothing." And Mark walked away, feeling very frustrated.

We need to stop, look, and listen when our kids talk to us. Stop what we are doing, make eye contact, and listen intently. In a survey of sixty high school seniors, the question was posed, "Is your mother/father a good listener?" Almost eighty percent responded that mom is a good listener, whereas less than half said that dad is a good listener. Adolescents need their dads to listen to them. It is one of the best ways that dads can build that close connection with their kids.

6. *Have the courage to be fully human.* Express genuine emotion. My dad never once cried in front of me while growing up. As a teenager, I would have emotional, heart-to-heart talks with my mom and would force myself to suppress my tears. Since I did not think it was manly to shed tears, I eventually taught myself not to. It took many years for me to re-learn the ability to cry. It is important for fathers to express the full range of human emotions—to laugh and cry, to be angry and sad, express frustration and joy, and to be strong and vulnerable. By doing so we are teaching our sons and daughters that "real men" can feel and express the whole range of emotions.

I realize that expressing emotions is not easy for many men. I used to think that this was all culturally and socially conditioned. But now I understand that there are physiological differences that make it difficult for many men to express their feelings. Because of the way that men's brains are wired, we are not as in touch with our feelings as most women are. But we *can* learn to be more in touch with our feelings, and it is important for both our intimacy with our wives and our modeling for our sons and daughters that we learn how to get in touch with and share our feelings.

Looking in the rearview mirror

It's not easy being a good dad, and the doubt and worry and fear can be painful. Feeling confident and being stripped of confidence are integral parts of the fathering process, a process filled with joyful times and occasional frustration, moments of self-doubt and times of self-confidence, moments of despair and worry, and moments of hope and expectation and pride. But at the end of the day, I find consolation in the words of a ten-year-old boy who once said, "Fathers are the greatest!"

Improving Your Parenting Partnership

The weather was warm and balmy that Sunday afternoon as we were driving out to the country to Escalon, a small farming community in California's central valley. We were on our way to have dinner with Rhonda and Tony. Rhonda was Patt's college roommate. Our weddings were a few months apart, and our friendship spans more than two decades.

Tony owns a dairy business and Rhonda is a nurse practitioner. They have two teenage sons. "We were Ozzie and Harriet parents before our boys became teenagers," recalled Rhonda. "We *never* argued about how to raise our kids. But when they turned thirteen, Tony and I couldn't agree at all; we had all kinds of arguments about how they should be raised!"

Marriage researchers tell us that when teenagers are in the home, there is the greatest likelihood of marital dissatisfaction. This isn't surprising. During the adolescent years, most couples experience greater conflict about how to discipline the kids.

In Steve's senior Marriage and Family class he assigns his students a project where they interview married couples. One of the questions is, "What do you argue about in your marriage?" The two most common answers are arguments over finances and disagreements about how to raise the kids.

It is not possible to completely avoid arguments, but there are ways to reduce the number of conflicts you engage in while parenting your adolescents. It is often a great chal-

> It is not possible to completely avoid arguments, but there are ways to reduce the number of conflicts you engage in while parenting your adolescents.

When the first parent says "no" and the other parent says "yes," it undermines the authority of the first parent.

lenge for parents to be on the same page with regard to discipline and raising adolescents. Larry, a high school senior wrote, "When I can get my parents to disagree, I can get anything I want."

Roger got his license the day after his sixteenth birthday. In California there is a law stating that for the first six months a new driver is not allowed to have a passenger in the car under the age of twenty-five. Roger and his parents knew the law. Mom was quite vocal about not allowing Roger to drive other kids within the sixth month period, so when Roger asked her if he could drive Michelle to the movies there was no debate. Then he wandered into the family room to work on Dad.

Roger told his dad the story: "Michelle's parents can't drive her to the theater, but they said that it would be okay for me to drive her, even though I just got my license." He reminded his dad of the one exception to the new law, "If you have a note from your parent and permission from the passenger's parent, you can drive someone under twenty-five. Michelle's parents said they'd write a note for her."

Dad hesitated. He did not feel totally comfortable with the idea, and his hesitation encouraged Roger to push more. "Dad, we aren't breaking the law and the movie's going to start soon. I need to leave now. What do you think? Can I drive her?"

"Oh, I guess it's okay," Dad said reluctantly. "I'll write you a note. Keep it in the glove box."

Roger rushed out of the house.

When Mom learned that Dad had given Roger permission to drive his girlfriend to the movies, she was furious with her husband. She felt betrayed and sabotaged by her parenting partner.

Good cop, bad cop

Being on the same page is challenging. When the first parent says "no" and the other parent says "yes," it undermines the authority of the first parent. This is a dangerous dynamic.

In some relationships, the husband is the stricter of the two, while the wife is more lenient. In other marriages, the wife is stricter than the husband. Whatever the case, when couples are not on the same wavelength with regard to disciplining their teens, it creates conflict.

When Paula and Bill argue about how to discipline their fourteen-year-old son, Paula tends to blame Bill, accusing him of not being strict enough. Soft-spoken Bill reacts by pouting, then refuses to talk, shunning his wife for days. Their disagreements begin to interfere with their being effective parents, as well as being a loving married couple. Both child and parents lose when animosity is present.

Every couple experiences misunderstandings and hurt as well as the good, cooperative, and fulfilling side of parenting. It is impossible for two people to agree completely on everything. This is because we have had different teachers. We tend to raise our kids the way we were raised.

Four tips for improving your parenting partnership:

1. *Be aware of how your history affects your parenting.* Without reflecting on your past history, unhealthy patterns of communication may repeat themselves in your relationships, both with your partner and with your kids. In some cases, a person may parent in a style that is the exact opposite of the way they were parented. Both extremes may be unhealthy.

   Growing up in the Saso family, I was raised in an authoritarian home with an emotionally distant father. He is no longer the same man as he was when I was a child, but I promised myself that when I became a father, I would be different. Unfortunately, the pendulum swung from one extreme to the other. Instead of finding a middle course, I became the exact opposite of my undemocratic dad. In the process of parenting our teenagers, my permissiveness has been the source of many conflicts with Patt. There have been occasions when I have undermined her authority by disagreeing with her directives or by not supporting her parenting decisions. I have gradually been learning to recognize this pattern when it arises (and she reminds me!), and I am making changes. Being united and working in partnership is important to me and it is important that our kids witness this partnership.

2. *Support your partner in his or her decisions.* When your partner makes a parenting decision, be supportive. Model healthy disagreements and problem solving techniques with your partner in front of your kids. As our story of the driver's license illustrates, when one parent tells the children one thing and the other parent tells them the opposite, it sabotages your partner, and undermines the parenting partnership.

   If your partner hands out a consequence that you do not agree with, support her decision. Then talk about it in private at a later time, as discussed in the next point.

3. *Discuss in private differences of opinion about how to discipline the kids.* When you disagree about how to handle a child-rearing issue, discuss it in private. Make an agreement on how to handle a particular situation, and then share your decision with the kids. When you are discussing the issue, try to be flexible and willing to compromise. Families function more calmly when each partner exercises a loving give-and-take on the rules. Do not impose your will on your partner. Remember that these two "C" words—consideration and collaboration—lead to a more stable relationship and home life.

4. *Gradually make the shift to a parenting partnership.* Making modifications in a family system requires patience. Change takes time. Expect protests. Let your kids witness you working in unison. And when the stress is up and the temptation arises to revert back to your old patterns, stay the course. Given time, your kids will respect the strength of your new family commitment, and they will recognize that you and your spouse are allies when it comes to discipline issues.

If you and your partner are in conflict on child-rearing practices, consider changing for the sake of the kids. Do not allow arguments over the kids to jeopardize your relationship. During the teen years when marital satisfaction is at its lowest point, do whatever it takes to keep your parenting partnership strong. Consider counseling if you are unable to resolve the problems on your own.

And, as a bonus: According to several empty nesters we know, after the teen years, marital satisfaction does return.

Relationship Matters

This may come as a surprise to you, but your sons and daughters want to spend more time with you. Mounting evidence indicates that increasing numbers of teens feel they are not getting enough time with parents.

Seventy-three percent of teenagers tell us that their parents do not spend enough time with them. That is what a *Newsweek* magazine poll in 2000 indicated. Our better-quicker-faster culture along with changes in the nuclear family have caught up with us. Parents strapped for time, real or imagined, by cultural expectations, work demands, single parenthood, and the like are unable to be there for their children in the way kids need and want.

Many parents think that teens don't want their input or company. When parents try to strike up a conversation with their teens, the response is often a grunt that can be interpreted as, "I hate you. Don't talk to me." William Pollack, author of *Real Boys*, writes:

> Although we are often taught that adolescents—especially male adolescents—need or want to separate from their families, this is another dangerous myth. Certainly adolescents are struggling with issues of identity and growth and will push at us, even push away from us, at times. Certainly they wish to spend some time away from home and develop an individual sense of self. But our sons and daughters rarely wish to cut their ties, be on their own, or separate from us.

Your teen's monosyllabic response is not an indication that he doesn't want to talk to you. It's just that he does not feel like talking right now, or doesn't yet know how.

Relationship before rules

Listen carefully. Your teenagers consider their relationship with you a high priority. And this relationship is key for their mental health.

The National Longitudinal Study of Adolescent Health (1997) found that:

> Teenagers who have emotional attachments to their parents and teachers are much less likely to use drugs and alcohol, attempt suicide, engage in violence, or become sexually active at an early age . . . feeling loved, understood and paid attention to by parents helps teenagers avoid risky activities regardless if a child comes from a one- or two-parent family.

Effective parenting is not about finding new ways to control our teens' behavior. It is about how to guide our kids into becoming their truest and best selves, independent from us. We do this through our relationships. The core of parenting is in the real relationship we cultivate with our kids. In our first book, *10 Best Gifts for Your Teen*, we write:

> The heart of successful parenting of teenagers is in the relationship we form with them. Building a relationship of mutual respect, love, and understanding, and providing support, consistency, structure, and limits—these are the foundations of effective parenting.

Being present to our teens and being there for them in a particular way, when it really matters most, is more important than the rules that we establish or try to enforce. If our primary energy goes toward the enforcement of rules, and not on teaching our children internal constraints, we can seriously damage the parent-teen relationship. Without relationships we have no solid foundation on which to build.

159

Three advantages of a bonded relationship between parent and child:

1. *Teens are less likely to engage in high-risk behaviors.* A 2002 study reported in the *Journal of Adolescent Health* substantiates the power and advantages of a close relationship between parent and teen. For example, the stronger the parent-teen relationship, the less likely your child is to have sex before he or she should. The type of connection identified in the study includes how well you communicate, how much you know about your child's friends, their friends' families, and what your teens watch, read, and do in their spare time.

   Another study conducted in 2000 by the President's Council of Economic Advisors found that teens who say that they feel close to at least one parent are far less likely to consider suicide or even to engage in antisocial behavior, such as fighting at school.

   Lynn McDonald, a psychologist at the University of Wisconsin's School of Education, says, "The two things that kids say that help them steer clear of trouble are a good relationship with parents and a good relationship with their school."

2. *Parents and teens are better able to work through crisis situations.* A second advantage of a close parent-teen relationship is that adolescents who have a strong connection to their parents have something to fall back on when crisis or conflict arises. A teenager who genuinely cares about her parents and whose parents care about her emotional security is more likely to work through problems, rather than to allow the problems to be a cause of severing the relationship.

   During her sophomore year in high school, Rita began experimenting with smoking marijuana. While putting clothes away in Rita's room, Mom discovered the marijuana. She was horrified. She had no idea that her daughter was involved with drugs. When she talked to her daughter about her distress and disappointment, Rita began to cry. She told her mom how sorry she was that she disappointed her and that she would stop. She didn't want to harm the trust that the two of them had with each other.

The relationship with her mother motivated her to work on the problem, rather than risk disapproval. Mom supported her daughter's efforts by better supervising Rita's activities. In this case the parent-teen relationship didn't prevent the risky behavior, but it certainly was an essential factor in addressing the issue and preventing more of the potentially dangerous involvement.

3. *Parents exercise influence in their teens' lives.* A third advantage of a strong parent-teen connection is that it affords an opportunity for the teenager to be influenced by his parents. Teens who feel unloved or neglected rarely seek out parental advice or guidance. Adolescents who feel cared for and understood by their parents tend to ask for their guidance. According to research conducted by the Search Institute, only one of out four teens surveyed said that they would go to their parents to seek advice or counsel.

One way parents can make themselves more approachable is by offering their kids "amnesty talks." An amnesty talk is an opportunity for kids in their formative years to talk to a parent about something personal and emotional, even something that they have done that is potentially incriminating, without the threat of reprisal or punishment.

The teen approaches the parent and asks if he may have an amnesty talk. If an adolescent asks for an amnesty talk, it means he needs to share something important. If the parent agrees, the kid tells his story. The parent is available during this time to help him identify what emotions he is feeling, so that he can learn how to control his own emotional states. The parent is free to offer input in the form of guidance, advice, or suggestions, but not to take punitive action. The teen has "amnesty" from disciplinary consequences.

Some parents tell us that there is no way that they can do this with their kids. Their own emotions of fear, anger, or embarrassment may be an obstacle to having an amnesty talk with their teens. They may not be able to listen without the need to punish. However, if you are willing to make amnesty talks available to your teenager, it may be that she will be more willing to talk to you than if she thinks you will punish her for what is being disclosed.

Be parents, not friends

Forming a strong parent-teen relationship does not mean that parents become friends with their adolescents. Teens, in fact, don't want their parents to be their friends. They have plenty of friends their own age. Kids hate it when parents try to act like teenagers or talk like them. My students tell me that they think it's strange when their dads act like teenagers, pointing out to them a cute girl or asking them if they "scored" any phone numbers after a school dance. What teens do want is a parent who will listen to them, guide them, love them, and ensure their safety. What they want is a parent who will establish fair rules and consequences, and will be evenhanded in applying them. They want a close relationship with their parents, but not to be "buddies" with them.

Teens, in fact, don't want their parents to be their friends. They have plenty of friends their own age.

Spend time with your kids, fostering a relationship based on mutual trust and respect, and enjoy the fruits of this important labor of love for years to come.

Teaching Emotional Intelligence

Rudy and his son Jesse were in a heated argument about driving privileges. Jesse wanted the car that night to go to his friend's house. A group of friends were getting together and he wanted to join them. Rudy told Jesse he couldn't use the car that night because he was being irresponsible about his chores. He pointed out that Jesse told him two days ago that he would mow the lawn, and it still was not done. Jesse responded with intense emotion, "You don't know me at all. I hate you, Dad. You're the worst parent ever."

Rudy took a deep breath. His son was really upset and Rudy knew enough not to take Jesse's words literally. "Jesse, I can see that you are really angry that I won't let you take the car tonight. And I'm feeling really frustrated that you gave me your word about mowing the lawn and it's still not done."

"I'm gonna mow it, Dad."

"I guess I need to know what your plan is. When are you intending to get your chore done?"

"If I mow it right now, can I have the car tonight?"

"Jess, I don't know. I still need to think about that."

"Well, if you're not going to let me take the car, then I'm not going to mow the lawn."

Rudy decided not to move into a power struggle with his son, but before leaving the room he said, "Jesse, we all have chores around the house. We all have to do our part to make our home comfortable for everyone. I appreciate what you do around here to help out, and your mom and I are very generous with helping you out. We'll talk about the car later today."

Many parents miss the opportunity to recognize the language of their child's emotions, especially in the heat of the moment. Identifying, labeling, and acknowledging your teenager's feelings is an opening for connection and learning. If you are angry, hostile, or disrespectful in return, or ignore, dismiss, or negate the underlying emotion, you will miss this opportunity.

As you might have guessed, Jesse mowed the lawn without a fuss. He apologized to his dad for yelling at him. It was a genuine apology, and Dad did let Jess take the car that night.

Emotion coaching

Recent scientific studies have shown that the ability to deal with feelings—even more than IQ—will determine a person's success and happiness in all areas of life, including relationships. The emotional health of your teenager has a significant impact on his long-term well-being. Emotional intelligence includes knowing what you are feeling, taking responsibility for your feelings, being able to talk about what you are feeling, and being able to self-soothe.

Acclaimed psychologist and researcher Dr. John Gottman in his book *Raising an Emotionally Intelligent Child*, writes, "Every parent knows the importance of equipping children with the intellectual skills they need to succeed in school and life. But children also need to master their emotions." Gottman's research suggests that parents need to be primed with the skills to be an "emotion coach." His five-step process teaches parents how to:

- be aware of a child's emotions,

- recognize emotional expression as an opportunity for intimacy and teaching,

- listen empathetically and validate a child's feelings,

- label emotions in words a child can understand, and

- help a child come up with an appropriate way to solve a problem or deal with an upsetting issue or situation.

Gottman says that kids who learn emotional awareness early in life are better able to motivate themselves, control impulses, delay gratification, read other people's social cues, and cope with life's ups and downs. He encourages parents to be "emotion affirming" rather than "emotion dismissing." Some parents want to protect their kids from negative emotions. If their child is depressed or sad or angry, these parents feel that it reflects negatively on them. They think they are bad parents because their kids are experiencing negative emotions.

> The emotional health of your teenager has a significant impact on his long-term well-being.

Emotion dismissing parents ignore, completely deny, or minimize their children's feelings. A classic example is the parent who responds to his five-year-old's fear of the dark by saying, "There's nothing to be afraid of. Now be a big boy and go back to bed." Some parents do the same thing with their teenagers. "Don't feel bad about not making the soccer team. You can always go out for track." Or, "Don't be sad that you broke up with your boyfriend; there are lots of other fish in the sea. Besides, I didn't like him anyway." These parents do not want their kids to experience negative emotions and to feel bad so they deny their very real feelings.

Emotion affirming parents are sensitive to lower intensity feelings in themselves and in their kids. They acknowledge and affirm their children's feelings, even the negative ones. They listen to their kids with empathy. An emotion affirming parent would say, "I can hear that you are afraid to make the phone call. Let's role play so you will feel more comfortable," or, "How painful for you not to make the soccer team. I know how much you wanted to make the team, and how hard you worked for this. You must be very disappointed. I am sad that you didn't make it."

Emotion affirming parents give their kids words for their emotions, which gives kids a sense of control. The child feels that she can do something about the feeling. The following are tips for parents to heighten their children's emotional awareness.

Four tips for fostering emotional intelligence:

1. *Become aware of your teenager's emotions.* Tune in to what your son or daughter is feeling. It doesn't help much to ask *what* they are feeling, since most teens cannot answer that question. Often they do not really know what they are feeling. Instead, become attuned to their feelings and feed back to them what you *think* they are feeling. "I sense that you are feeling overwhelmed with your school obligations right now." Or, "I know you said that it's no big deal, but you must be disappointed that you got cut from the team. You're a good player, and it's hurtful not to have your skills recognized."

2. *Recognize the emotion as an opening for caring and teaching.* Use the emotional experience of your teenager as an opportunity to teach. "Breaking up with a girlfriend can be very painful. The hurt that you are feeling now is in proportion to the loving feelings that you developed for your girlfriend. A good way to heal, but not an easy way, is to allow yourself to let the pain in and really feel the loss. Eventually, you will be able to let it go."

3. *Listen empathetically, validating your child's feelings.* Sometimes it is not easy to do this because our teens' feelings sometimes seem out of proportion to the triggering event. When our son Brian was in seventh grade, he earned an A- on his report card in math. He was used to getting straight A's. He was extremely upset and disappointed. We didn't say, "Why are you so upset? It's still a good grade." Even though we

> Emotionally intelligent kids are better able to calm themselves, bounce back from adversity, and carry on with productive activities.

were happy with the grade, Brian was not. So we validated his feelings: "It's frustrating and disappointing when you get a grade that is less than what you wanted. You worked hard, and were expecting an A rather than an A-. We are proud of you, and want you to know that we understand your disappointment."

4. *Set limits while exploring strategies to solve the problem at hand.* Being emotion affirming does not mean tolerating disrespect or rudeness from your adolescent. Your teenager has every right to express her feelings, but she does not have the right to throw them in your face. Help your daughter to move from "I hate you" to "I am really pissed at you" to "I am feeling incredibly angry right now."

Any parent can learn to become an emotional teacher. Parents who "emotion coach" their kids still have children who get sad, angry, or scared under difficult circumstances, but these emotionally intelligent kids are better able to calm themselves, bounce back from adversity, and carry on with productive activities.

Teaching children to master their emotions helps them to have greater self-confidence, perform better in school, and have better social interactions and friendships. When we are civil and connect with our children on a real and emotional level, and are genuinely interested in their world, it enriches the bonds we have with them and esteems them. And it contributes immensely to the healthy development of our next generation of adults.

Giving Thanks for Our Kids

Do you remember that minivan bumper sticker, "Have You Hugged Your Kids Today?"

As parents we concern ourselves with the nitty-gritty in our roles as mother or father, making sure our kids have good friends, wanting them to study hard and do well in school, keeping them involved in activities, and continually evaluating if they are going in the right direction. We spend time trying to figure out the correct logical consequences for this or that misbehaver. We lose sleep with worry.

In all the rush, we sometimes forget what is most important. We lose sight of the precious gifts our children are, and fail to show them how much we love them. We need a bumper sticker to remind us to hug our kids and tell them that we love them.

Family traditions

Every year during the Christmas season our family gathers with friends to read aloud *A Christmas Carol* by Charles Dickens. It is a tradition that began ten years ago, and one that our kids still eagerly look forward to each December. Young and old, we gather to recall once again the Ghost of Christmas Past and the miraculous transformation of Mr. Scrooge's heart. His heart had hardened, and he became insensitive to the needs of others. After focusing on material success for so many years, he was given a second chance to love again.

The holiday season is an obvious time to express love and appreciation for others, but what about right now? While getting ready to finish up a phone conversation with my mom recently, I said, "I love you, Mom."

"Babe, you know I love you," was her response.

She couldn't say the words I longed to hear. "You know I love you" is not saying the same thing. Children, even adult children, need to hear the words "I love you" spoken genuinely. Children not only need to hear these words, but they need to be shown love and affection as well.

> Children, even adult children, need to hear the words "I love you" spoken genuinely.

Model ways for the family to show love to one another:

- *Write your teen a letter.* This can be a letter of thanks, telling him what you like and appreciate about him, and what you especially love about him.

- *Go on an outing together.* One-on-one time with each child is important. In a recent "Dear Carolyn" column a twin girl writes: "I really love my dad, but he has little interest in doing things with me. He spends lots of time with my brother every weekend, taking him to ballgames and playing golf and tennis with him, and they go on camping trips in the summer, but he never invites me. . . . I don't think he understands how much it hurts."

- *Make a special meal.* In our home we have a special breakfast. To celebrate holidays and birthdays we make German pancakes! The person we are celebrating is served on a decorated plate that has the words, "You are special today" written on it. It is a simple way of acknowledging an accomplishment or of saying we notice you and love you.

Christmas every day

Pat Desmond, a longtime friend of Steve's, tells a story about his younger sister Monica and how she broke her older brother of the habit of teasing her. Together they decided that whenever he would begin teasing, she would whisper, "Pat, it's Christmas," and this would be a reminder to him to stop picking on his sister.

Let's develop the same awareness with regard to our kids and remind ourselves that every day is Christmas. Every day is a day for celebrating our kids, for gifting them with words of praise and encouragement. Instead, what many of us do is bombard our kids with criticism and negativity. Self-esteem researchers report that the average parent hands out eighteen putdowns for every "put-up." Eighteen critical comments for every one word of praise and affirmation! Let's strive to reverse those numbers by making every day a Christmas day.

Four opportunities to affirm kids every day of the year:

1. *Give your teenager words of encouragement.* The word "encourage" comes from the French root *cour* which means "heart." When we encourage our kids, we give them heart. When we discourage, we remove their heart. Sometimes our kids lose heart because we are overly critical. A parent recently shared with me how upset she was about her daughter's grade point average. It had "fallen" from a 4.33 to a 4.17. I couldn't believe what I was hearing. Instead of criticizing, focus on what your kids are doing well, not simply their successes, but their hard work, growth as persons, or improvement in behavior, cooperation, or schoolwork.

> Instead of criticizing, focus on what your kids are doing well, not simply their successes, but their hard work, growth as persons, or improvement in behavior, cooperation, or schoolwork.

As a sophomore, Paul had an extremely hard time getting up and ready for school in the morning. We had to call him several times before he would drag himself out of bed just in time to join the carpool. When he got his license we expected that this behavior would continue. We were concerned because he would be driving the carpool the following school year. However, miracles do happen. When school started that fall, Paul made a wondrous transformation. He set his alarm clock and got himself up and out the door without even one wake-up call or reminder from us. When we trusted him with more responsibility he proved to us he could handle it. After a few weeks, we acknowledged his new responsible behavior, "Paul, we are so proud of you, the way you have been getting yourself up in the morning on your own. It shows a real growth in maturity and that you are dependable. Keep up the good work."

2. *At the end of the day.* Look for something to affirm in each member of the family every day. Bedtime is a perfect opportunity. Our hearts are open in a different way at night. We tend to be more receptive to words of love and appreciation.

   Larry tells his daughter, "Rebecca, I am so glad that you are my daughter. You are a precious gift to me. I love you so much. I know that you are going to make a significant difference in the world. Whatever you choose to do, I know that by your efforts you will make the world a better place."

   Ken sometimes feels apprehension. When he is heading for bed and passes his son's bedroom, he finds it rather difficult to say, "I love you." Sometimes he says simply "goodnight," while at other times he will summon up the courage to say a quick, "Love you, Tommy." It can be awkward, especially for men, to reach out and say tender words to sons. By contrast, he has no trouble at all saying "I love you" to his teenage daughter. So what he sometimes does is write a note. It is easier to express his thoughts on paper. Recently he wrote: "Son, thanks for driving your sister to volleyball practice after school today. I appreciate your generosity. I love you. Love, Dad."

3. *Reconcile.* Teenagers need to hear affirming and loving words during times of conflict. When there has been

damage done to the relationship, work toward healing it. Talking on a heart level opens the door for communication, love, and understanding.

Julie confides that when she is angry at her son's behavior she withdraws her love. "I don't want him to think that what he did is okay with me." What her son needs to hear is: "Joe, I was really upset when you went out after I told you not to. I apologize for jumping to conclusions and yelling at you. I was scared to death when you walked out of the house that late. I had no idea where you were going and was worried about your safety. I don't want anything to happen to you. I was really unaware of how upset you were. Next time I hope that we can talk about what is going on for each of us rather than have you leave the house in anger."

4. *Hug your kids.* Some teens are very open to being hugged by their parents, while others are not. One mom complained, "I started to give my seventh grade son a hug, and he pushed me away. I was so hurt. He always used to hug me." Although this is fairly normal teenage developmental behavior, it can be very painful and frustrating. But this does not mean that all teens will recoil from a parent's touch. In fact some adolescents, males as well as females, don't mind being shown physical affection by their parents. Take the cue from your teen as to the appropriateness of physical affection.

When our daughter began middle school, as her father, I prepared myself for the likelihood that she would not feel comfortable with me hugging her during her teen years. To my surprise, she has not been reluctant to hug me or let me put my arm around her shoulder. She is comfortable with physical affection. Our sons definitely did not want to be hugged or even touched much during their early teen years. So we respected their needs and space. Now that Brian is in college, he is once again hugging Mom and Dad.

Whether it be the holiday season or ordinary time, it is vitally important that we affirm and appreciate our kids. We need to show and tell them the love we have for them. Our kids need expressions of affection to develop a healthy self-esteem and to grow into happy and healthy adults. So don't wait for the holiday season to give thanks for your kids. Give thanks for them every day. Write that bumper sticker on your heart.

Hey, have you hugged your kids today?

Leading Like a Parent

Michael is a fifteen-year-old sophomore. His dad teaches history at the same high school he attends. There was an in-service day for the teachers, so the students had the day off. Michael spent his day sleeping and playing on the computer.

At 3:30, when Michael's father returned home from school, he asked his son if he had begun working on the term paper due for his English class. The young man replied, "I mostly just chilled in my room and played on the computer. I didn't get to the term paper." The father was frustrated that his son hadn't used his time more wisely.

"I thought you would use the day off from school to get a head start on your paper," suggested the father.

"Well, I guess you thought wrong."

Michael's father later told us that if he had said that to *his* father, "He would have slapped me into next week."

How would you respond?

We live in an incredibly disrespectful culture, and our kids are products of this culture. It is no secret to parents of adolescents that teens are more mouthy and disrespectful than kids were even a generation ago. We hear many parents saying, "I would never have spoken to my parents the way my teen speaks to me."

Some parents respond to the disrespectful comments of their teens by themselves being disrespectful by labeling or calling their kids names, for example:

- "You are nothing but a selfish, spoiled brat."

- "You are a pain in the butt."

- "I wish you were never born."

- "What a wimp."

Other parents punish the disrespect by grounding or taking away privileges.

Michael's dad let his son know very clearly that this was no way to talk to a parent, and that he felt disrespected by what Michael had said. Michael was surprised by his father's words, because he did not intend his words to be disrespectful. Nonetheless, Michael's father told his son that in the future he expected him to think before he speaks and to concentrate on being more respectful in his words and actions.

Some parents find this response unsatisfying. They want to know what else to do. One father wrote: "Our fifteen-year-old son has played that scene out many times, practically verbatim. I know that I could say 'I feel that you are not being respectful when you speak to me like that' . . . but then what?"

Most of the time, this is all a parent needs to do. If the disrespect is flagrant or repeated, then an appropriate disciplinary consequence may be in order, such as grounding for a Friday evening or suspending driving privileges for a day or two.

Modeling respectful behavior

What teens need today more than anything is a model of respectful behavior. When disrespected by our teenagers, we can do three very important things:

- Stay calm and firm.

- Let our kids know that it is not okay to speak to us disrespectfully.

- Return respect for the disrespect.

In this way we are giving our kids a model for the kinds of behaviors we want and expect from them.

While speaking about "Responsible Sexuality" to a local high school youth group, I invited the students to write their questions on 3 x 5 cards. These questions were to be answered after the break. One of the student comments was particularly upsetting. On the card were written the words,

"You don't know shit." My first reaction was complete shock, and my next reaction was sadness for the disrespectful culture that spawned such a response. I read the "question" aloud to the group, and then responded, "I am very hurt by this disrespectful comment. If you disagree with what I have said here tonight, you are certainly free to voice your disagreement. But to address me in such a disrespectful manner is both immature and inappropriate."

Respect: look again

The word respect comes from the Latin *respectare*, which means to "look at again." When we respect someone, we look at them a second time. We look past their behavior, which may be annoying and hurtful, in order to see the deeper message being sent. This can take great patience and great courage on parents' part. It may help to remind ourselves that disrespectful behavior can mask deeper emotions. Often our kids are afraid, overwhelmed, unsure, and confused. Growing up is hard to do.

To respect our teens is to look past their outrageous and sometimes hurtful comments and see the inner person, the person worthy of dignity and respect. We need to look past the occasional stinging words and out-of-control emotions in order to see the struggling child whom we love and who needs to learn more effective communication skills.

The gift that keeps on giving

The first and most important ingredient in being a loving parent is respect. It is the foundation of all strong, loving relationships. When we show respect for our kids, eventually the respect is returned and it comes full circle. It is truly the gift that keeps on giving.

It is not always easy to parent in a respectful manner. It is far easier to "slap them into next week." It takes strength of character to return respect for disrespect. The choice is ours.

The Secret Power Behind Setting Goals

One summer while still in college, I was hired as a carpenter building track homes. It paid well and the money was needed for college. There were only two females on the crew, and I was one of them. Being a newbie, I was more of a gopher than a carpenter. I had to "go for" this and go for that to help out the seasoned carpenters. But as my skills improved, I became more of a carpenter.

A carpenter would never conceive of building a house without blueprints. "Plan your work and work your plan" is what my brother-in-law used to say. Follow the blueprints and you will reach your goal. Goal-setting gives us a direction. And we can decide that direction by choosing what goals to set.

There is tremendous power in setting goals, a force that parents can teach to their teenagers. Goal-setting develops a sense of empowerment. It teaches responsibility and perseverance. The unspoken message received is that you can make things happen in your life, rather than wait for things to happen. Coaching our teens to set goals for themselves demonstrates that they can have some control over their own destiny in life.

We have been keeping a list of goals for years. Together, we establish one-year, five-year, and ten-year goals, goals for our business and family, as well as individual goals. Once or twice a year we revisit them. What never ceases to amaze us is how many of these goals get accomplished without being fully aware of the effort it took in completing them.

> Coaching our teens to set goals for themselves demonstrates that they can have some control over their own destiny in life.

Six tips in coaching your teenagers to set goals:

1. *Model for your kids the power of goal-setting.* I had always wanted to hike to the top of Half Dome in Yosemite National Park. Patt wasn't so sure that this old body could make it! I first set this goal for myself in 1997 and included it in my New Year's Resolutions every year after that. Finally, in the summer of 2004, along with Patt and several friends, I made the seventeen-mile trek, ascending 5,000 feet above sea level. Upon reaching the top, I felt a tremendous sense of satisfaction and accomplishment.

   Our kids knew that this was a goal I had set for myself. On the calendar, circled in red ink, was the departure day, and months before, the training program began. There were times when my teenagers joined me on my workouts. They were fully aware of my goal and they witnessed the effort it took to accomplish it. It didn't just happen by a stroke of luck; they saw me make it happen. I was able to model for them the power of setting goals.

2. *Write down your goals on paper.* One secret of accomplishing goals is to write them down. Consciously and intentionally record your dreams and desires, and then share them out loud. Once you do, most goals seem to come to fruition almost effortlessly. They may not be accomplished in your time frame, but almost all goals recorded eventually are met.

3. *Encourage your teenager to set personal goals.* Goal-setting teaches a young person how to plan ahead and make choices. It is an excellent way to teach your kids about responsibility, perseverance, and a sense of accomplishment and personal satisfaction. It is a crucial social competency needed for success in later life.

   A few years ago, our daughter asked us for a pet. She wanted a cockatiel. We encouraged Mikhaila to work toward the goal of buying a cockatiel with her own money. That summer we had a huge project to strip the wallpaper from several walls in our home. Mikhaila gladly took on the tedious job of stripping wallpaper. She also cleaned a neighbor's house and took care of people's pets. She earned enough money from the jobs to buy a cage and eventually her birds. She ended up buying two, so they could keep each other company. She was very proud of herself and certainly felt a great sense of accomplishment from not only setting and reaching her goal, but exceeding it.

4. *Help your teenager to set academic goals.* At the beginning of every new grading period we sit down with our kids individually and ask them what kind of grades they want to earn. Goals must be realistic. Then we ask them what they need to do to accomplish them. They might say they need to complete all their homework assignments, or to keep up with the required reading, or to be more disciplined about studying for tests. One time our junior asked for tutoring to help him get the grade he wanted in chemistry. Another time our daughter asked the teacher for extra credit work. It all gets written down and posted near their desks. At the end of the quarter we re-evaluate to assess what worked and what didn't. What our kids learn is that they earn their grades by the effort they put forth, not by being lucky or by being the teacher's pet. Grades are earned, not given. For more about achieving success in the classroom, read the chapter "Helping Your Teenager Succeed in School" (pages 106–115).

5. *Set a family goal.* There is nothing more exciting than working on a collective goal as a team. In October, Mike and Marylou set a goal of saving up for a summer trip to Hawaii with the family. Everyone got involved. Through the months that followed, the kids saw their parents budgeting, saving, and making plans. The parents posted chore charts for each of the children, and with each chore completed it added money toward the

trip. That summer, the whole family enjoyed the rewards of another goal attained.

6. *Track progress.* Charting the progress of goal attainment can be fun and keeps people focused and motivated to reach the goal. The high school where I teach holds an annual magazine drive. There are countless incentives for the students to participate in the drive. I offer my own unique incentive by drawing a huge thermometer on a poster board, and hanging it on the classroom wall. On the very top of the thermometer is written the fund-raising goal for the class. The goal is always set higher than I think the class will be able to reach. Year after year, the class exceeds my expectations.

In the book *The 7 Habits of Highly Effective People,* Stephen Covey writes, "Begin with the end in mind." Successful people set goals for themselves. They are able to think about tomorrow and recognize what kind of effect their actions today can have on their future. They learn that things don't just happen by luck, but by hard work and focused attention. Ask your teenagers what they would like to accomplish. Write down their goals, read and revisit them. You may be amazed at what can be accomplished by applying the secrets of goal-setting.

Teaching Moral Awareness

The topic Monday morning in Marriage and Family class was "how to refuse a date without hurting the other person's feelings." The majority of the guys said that they would lie to the girl. They would say something like:

- "I already have a girlfriend."
- "I am busy that night."
- "I will be out of town."

"Why lie? Why not tell the truth?" I wanted to know. "Why not say something like, 'I'm not interested in going out with you. We can be friends, but I'm not interested in a dating relationship.'"

"Mr. Saso, nobody says that."

During this discussion one of the students said that there was nothing wrong with lying to a girl, since it really wasn't a very important issue. Mark continued, "Like last week when I was called into the Dean's office for not having the signature page signed that said that my parents and I had read the handbook. I told Mrs. Shanley that I had turned it in. I swore to her that I turned in the page. Mrs. Shanley believed me, and I didn't get a detention. So what's wrong with that? If it had been something important, I wouldn't have lied, but this was such a small thing, the lie was no big deal."

So I asked the class, "What do you guys think about this incident? What's wrong with what he did?" Nobody spoke out. Not a single senior in that class had the courage to say that what he did was wrong.

I challenged Mark. "What about your personal integrity? How can you live with yourself when you do something like that? What about the value of trust?" He repeated that if it were an important thing, he certainly would have told the truth, but this was such a small thing, and nobody got hurt by it. Mark did what so many people do when they want to justify their actions, rationalizing that "It's no big deal."

Theodore Roosevelt was quoted as saying, "To educate a person in mind and not in morals is to educate a menace to society." When facing moral challenges, before we can do what is right, we need the ability to judge what is right. Making moral decisions involves the ability to be aware of situations that require a moral judgment, to take into account the perspective of those who will be affected, and to assess your strengths, motives, and weaknesses.

Good character defined

Character is listening to your conscience and putting your values into action. Experiments on moral decision-making have shown that everyone has a conscience, one element of good character, even if they don't always follow it. It takes integrity and courage to do what is right in certain situations.

Educator Thomas Lickona states that character involves knowing what is right, caring about what is right, and doing what is right, even in the face of external pressure and temptation from within. Character development involves three more C's: conscience, compassion, and courage.

A person of character follows her conscience, which is the faculty that knows what is right, and feels obligated to do what is right. A person of character has compassion, which means that she has the ability to see things from the other person's point of view—a virtue that very few teenagers possess—and has empathy toward others. And a person of character has courage, which means that she is able to act on her values and do the right thing, even in the face of peer pressure or temptations, or even if no one is watching.

Three ways parents can nurture character in their children:

1. *Act morally.* If we want to help our children to become men and women of character, then we must be models of character. To instill in our teens strong character we need to live as persons of character.

   Driving to work one morning, I realized that my briefcase was sitting on the desk in our home office. Making a U-turn to return home, my cup of hot coffee tipped over. Instinctively, I reached down to grab it and when I looked up, I collided with a neighbor's parked car. My neighbor's car suffered a barely noticeable scratch, and my car had a smashed headlight.

   No one had witnessed the accident. I have to confess that it was tempting not to simply drive away. But I didn't. When I walked in the front door of our house, Patt and the kids could see that something was wrong. "What happened, Dad?" I told my family about hitting the neighbor's car.

   "I hit a parked car. My coffee spilled, and I bent down to pick it up and ran into the car. I need to go next door and let them know what happened." Our kids witnessed the whole thing. They saw me make a moral decision to do the right thing.

2. *Instill in your children the desire to do the right thing.* Teach not only by example, but also with words. When our daughter was in elementary school she and her friend wrote a mean anonymous letter to Gina. When Gina read the letter she confronted Mikhaila and expressed how hurtful it was to read it. Khaila denied and denied having anything to do with it, and because it wasn't in her handwriting there was no evidence to indicate she was involved.

> To instill in our teens strong character we need to live as persons of character.

Two days later, Khaila admitted to Patt that she had helped write the letter. She listened to her conscience. She was embarrassed and felt remorseful, and wanted to do the right thing. "Khaila, you need to go down to Gina's house and apologize."

Mikhaila was terrified. "Couldn't you tell her that I'm sorry?"

Patt insisted that she take responsibility for her actions and apologize in person. Patt role-played with Mikhaila what she might say. Together they walked down to Gina's house and apologized. Gina appreciated the apology and told Khaila that she had a lot of courage for talking to her face-to-face. This incident taught Mikhaila great lessons, among them the fact that she could summon the courage to admit her mistakes, ask for forgiveness, and repair a broken friendship.

3. *Act in loving, respectful ways toward your kids.* Another way that you can parent for character development is by loving your kids, even when you don't feel like it. There are plenty of times when I just don't like my kids. They are selfish or refuse to help out around the house. They are constantly quarreling and hassling one another. At times like these I just don't feel like acting lovingly toward them.

Lickona says that the most basic form of moral education is the treatment we receive. If we treat our kids in kind, respectful, loving ways, we are teaching them to be moral people. He writes, "Parents have the greatest moral impact when they provide, in the context of a caring relationship, both a good example and a reasoned advocacy of good values."

These are some of the ways that we can teach our kids to have strong character, to be people of conscience, compassion, and courage. It is a great challenge, given the cultural climate of today, but the rewards are great.

We leave you with some final words of wisdom by an anonymous author:

Watch your thoughts, they become words.

Watch your words, they become actions.

Watch your actions, they become habits.

Watch your habits, they become character.

Watch your character, it becomes your destiny.

Bibliography

Bayard, Robert and Jean Bayard. *How to Deal with Your Acting-Up Teenager*. New York: M. Evans and Co. Inc, 1981.

Bluestein, Jane. *Parents, Teens and Boundaries: How to Draw the Line*. Deerfield Beach, Florida: Health Communications, Inc., 1993.

Bradley, Michael J. *Yes, Your Teen Is Crazy*. Washington: Harbor Press, 2003.

Canter, Lee with Marlene Canter. *Assertive Discipline for Parents*. New York: Harper & Row Publishers, 1988.

Center for Disease Control and Prevention. World AIDS Day, 1997. Resource Booklet.

Coburn, Karen and Madge Treeger. *Letting Go: A Parents' Guide to Understanding the College Years*. New York: HarperCollins Publishers, 2003.

Cole, Deborah D. and Maureen Gallagher Duran. *Sex and Character*. Richardson, Texas: Pandas Publications, 1998.

Coloroso, Barbara. *Kids Are Worth It!* New York: Avon Books, 1994.

Deak, JoAnn. *Girls Will Be Girls: Raising Confident and Courageous Daughters*. New York: Hyperion, 2002.

"Do Kids Have Too Much Power?" *Time*, August 6, 2001. Vol. 63, No. 4. New York: Time, Inc.

Eastman, Meg. *Taming the Dragon in Your Child: Solutions for Breaking the Cycle of Family Anger*. New York: John Wiley & Sons, Inc., 1994.

Elium, Jeanne and Don Elium. *Raising a Daughter: Parents and the Awakening of a Healthy Woman*. California: Berkeley, California: Celestial Arts, 1994.

Elkind, David. *The Hurried Child*. Cambridge, Massachusetts: Perseus Publishing, 2001.

Ginott, Haim. *Between Parent and Child*. New York: Avon, 1965.

Glenn, H. Stephen and Jane Nelsen. *Raising Children for Success*. Fair Oaks, California: Sunrise Press, 1987.

Goleman, Daniel. *Emotional Intelligence*. New York: Bantam Books, 1995.

Gottman, John. *Raising an Emotionally Intelligent Child*. New York: Simon & Schuster, Inc., 1997.

Gottman, John M. and Joan DeClaire. *The Relationship Cure.* New York: Three Rivers Press, 2001.

Gray, John. *What You Feel You Can Heal.* Mill Valley, California: Heart Publishing Company, 1984.

Kelly, Kate. *The Complete Idiot's Guide to Parenting a Teenager.* Indianapolis: Alpha Books, 1996.

Kindlon, Dan and Michael Thompson. *Raising Cain: Protecting the Emotional Life of Boys.* New York: Ballantine Books, 2000.

Lickona, Thomas. *Educating for Character.* New York: Bantam Books, 1991.

Manning, Martha. *The Common Thread: Mothers, Daughters, and the Power of Empathy.* New York: HarperCollins Publishers, 2002.

McGraw, Phillip C. *Self Matters: Creating Your Life from the Inside Out.* New York: Simon & Schuster, 2001.

McKay, Matthew, Martha Davis, and Patricia Fanning. *Messages: The Communication Skills Book.* Oakland, California: New Harbinger Publications, 1983.

National Longitudinal Study of Adolescent Health. *The Journal of the American Medical Association.* The quote was taken from an article in the *San Jose Mercury News,* September 10, 1997.

Nezu, Christine and Arthur Nezu. *Awakening Self-Esteem.* Oakland, California: New Harbinger Publications, Inc., 2003.

"Parenting Practices at the Millennium," a study conducted by Dan Kindlon, professor of psychology at Harvard University.

Pearson, Carol. *Awakening the Heroes Within: Twelve Archetypes to Help Us Find Ourselves and Transform Our World.* New York: HarperCollins Publishers, 1991

Pollack, William. *Real Boys: Rescuing Our Sons from the Myths of Boyhood.* New York: Random House, 1998.

Rainey, Dennis and Barbara Rainey. *Parenting Today's Adolescent.* Nashville, Tennessee: Thomas Nelson, Inc. 1998.

Riera, Michael. *Staying Connected to Your Teenager.* Cambridge, Massachusetts: Perseus Publishing, 2003.

Riera, Michael and Joseph Di Prisco. *Field Guide to the American Teenager.* Cambridge, Massachusetts: Perseus Publishing, 2000.

Saso, Patt and Steve Saso. *10 Best Gifts for Your Teen.* Notre Dame, Indiana: Sorin Books, 1999.

Search Institute Publication, "The Asset Approach: Giving Kids What They Need to Succeed," 1997 by the Search Institute, 700 S. Third Street, Minneapolis, Minnesota 55415.

"Secrets of the Teen Brain," *Time*, May 10, 2004. Vol. 163, No. 19. New York: Time, Inc.

Siegel, Daniel and Mary Hartzell. *Parenting from the Inside Out*. New York: Penguin Group, Inc. 2003.

Shapiro, Lawrence E. *How to Raise a Child with a High EQ: A Parents' Guide to Emotional Intelligence*. New York: HarperCollins Publishers, Inc., 1997.

Smith, Manuel J. *When I Say No, I Feel Guilty*. New York: Bantam Books, 1975.

Stenzel, Pam. *Sex Has a Price Tag: Discussions About Sexuality, Spirituality, and Self-Respect*. Grand Rapids, Michigan: Zondervan Books, 2003.

"Teenager Craves Time with Father." Dear Carolyn Column, *San Jose Mercury News*, Sunday, April 24, 2005. Knight Ridder Publishing Company.

Walsh, David. *Why Do They Act That Way?* New York: Free Press, 2004.

Wolf, Anthony E. *Get Out of My Life But First Could You Drive Me and Cheryl to the Mall?* New York: The Noonday Press, 1991.

"Young Teens and Sex," *People*, January 31, 2005. Vol. 63, No. 4. New York: Time, Inc.

Sources for chapter on "Sex Education Begins at Home"

Fleming P, Byers RH, Sweeney PA, et al. HIV prevalence in the United States, 2000 [Abstract 11]. Presented at the Ninth Conference on Retroviruses and Opportunistic Infections, Seattle, WA; February 24–28, 2002.

CDC HIV/AIDS Surveillance Report: HIV Infection and AIDS in the United States, 2003.

Sources for chapter on "Teens and Marijuana"

Treatment Episodes Data Statistics, 1992–2002, SAMHA, 2004.

Cannabis Youth Treatment Randomized Field Experiment, preliminary report. U.S. Department of Health and Human Services, 2002.

W. Hall, N. Solowij, and J. Lemon. "The health and psychological consequences of cannabis use," (National Drug Strategy Monograph No. 25), Australian Government Publication Services, 1994.

Monitoring the Future National Results on Adolescent Drug Use: Overview of Key Findings 2002—Table 5.

A Note from the Authors

We hope that you have gained inspiration, hope, a few good laughs, and some practical strategies for parenting your teenagers from reading this book. Every parent of a teenager knows what a challenge it is to relate calmly and react even-handedly to a teenager's often bewildering and sometimes challenging behavior. We want to point out that in addition to this book, we have authored several other resources to support you in your parenting journey. Our parenting products will support you in raising caring, competent, and resilient teenagers.

Our first book, *10 Best Gifts for Your Teen* (Sorin Books), is an excellent guide for parents of younger teens and pre-teens, ages ten years and older. It is now published in five languages around the world. In addition, we have eight audio programs in both cassette and CD format. Some of our titles include: "How to Reduce Conflict between You and Your Teenager," "Fathering Teenagers," and "The Onset of Adolescence: Managing Your Changing Child." You can order the audio programs through our website at www.SasoSeminars.com.

In our parenting seminars and keynote addresses we show parents how to reduce conflict with their teen by relating when needed and relenting when necessary, offering support without infringing on their child's burgeoning sense of freedom. Using humor and real life anecdotes from the parenting trenches, our seminars are educational and entertaining.

Thank you for entrusting to us the privilege of supporting you as you parent your teenagers with T.L.C.

For more information about parenting resources or to book a seminar, visit us at:

www.SasoSeminars.com
e-mail: seminars@saso.com
408-262-6837